NOW AND AT THE
HOUR OF OUR DEATH

NOW AND
AT THE HOUR OF
OUR DEATH

Susana Moreira Marques

Translated by
Julia Sanches

LONDON · NEW YORK

First published in English translation in 2015 by And Other Stories
London – New York
www.andotherstories.org

First published as *Agora e na Hora da Nossa Morte* in 2012
by Edições Tinta da China, Lisbon, Portugal

ISBN 9781908276629
eBook ISBN 9781908276636

Editors: Ana Fletcher and Stefan Tobler; Copy-editor: Lucie Elven;
Proofreader: Alex Billington; Typesetter: Tetragon, London;
Typefaces: Linotype Swift Neue and Verlag; Cover Design:
Hannah Naughton; Cover Photograph: André Cepeda.

A catalogue record for this book is available from the British Library.

This book has been selected to receive financial assistance from English
PEN's PEN Translates! programme. English PEN exists to promote
literature and our understanding of it, to uphold writers' freedoms
around the world, to campaign against the persecution and imprisonment
of writers for stating their views, and to promote the friendly co-operation
of writers and the free exchange of ideas. www.englishpen.org

Supported using public funding by Arts Council England. Also funded
by the Direção-Geral do Livro, dos Arquivos e das Bibliotecas.

Supported using public funding by

**ARTS COUNCIL
ENGLAND**

GOVERNO DE
PORTUGAL

SECRETÁRIO DE ESTADO
DA CULTURA

CONTENTS

In 2009, the Calouste Gulbenkian Foundation launched a home palliative care project in the Planalto Mirandês, in Trás-os-Montes, a remote region in the north-east of Portugal.

A doctor, nurses, and other healthcare professionals travel from village to village helping dozens of patients of varying age, social class, and family circumstances to live the end of their lives in as much comfort as possible, and to die in company, at home.

This book is the result of several visits to this project and to these people, which all took place between June and October 2011.

TRAVEL NOTES
ABOUT DEATH

Does the road wind up-hill all the way?
Yes, to the very end.

CHRISTINA ROSSETTI
'Up-hill'

And Death is an eagle
whose cries no one describes.

CECÍLIA MEIRELES
'Posthumous Song'

There are things that can't be written about as they have been in the past. Something changes. First the eyes, then the heart – or senses, or whatever our ancestors called the soul – and, finally, the hands.

*

The first notes I take are about a man who was born, grew up, worked, was married, had a daughter, grew old, and died in the same village. These notes are not actually about the man, or his life, but about his death. They go like this:

Life in this house and with this family takes place entirely in this ground-level room, which is pleasingly dark and cool, and where there is a stove, a large table, an *escanho* – a long wooden bench common to Trás-os-Montes – and a door that leads to the pantry where they keep their produce.

It was April, the fireplace was not lit, but it was beside the fireplace that the man would often tell stories and where, all of a sudden full of life, he told stories that night. He said goodbye to his family – his daughter and granddaughter had come from the city. He said goodnight. He reminded the woman he'd been married to for sixty years to take her medicine.

The village where the man was born, grew up, worked, was married, had a daughter, grew old, and died is quaint, with its sculpted cross and renovated stone houses. It is tidy, clean. Quiet and very empty. It resembles a museum.

The widow, black shawl and unreadable face, moves slowly, bent by arthritis. She walks the streets like a shadow. She knows she is living the end of an era, of a way of life. When we are all gone, she says – meaning the old people – the shadows, the deserted houses will fall, slowly, and there will no longer be a village.

*

'We have a great history, the best weather in the world, and the best people in the world,' says a listener on the radio. 'We will raise our country up.'

The road runs on, spent. Old paths and, in the distance, the border. More and more, I have the feeling of being on an island. It was easier to get here than it will be to leave.

*

A.'s house or place of rest: an unmade bed, a cluttered bedside table, a radio, dirty laundry; a sheet hung from a rope separates the toilet from the rest of the room, whose floors and ceiling are bare.

A., or a man simply passing through life: parka, baseball cap, cheeks ruddy from drinking, steady eyes, hands rolling a cigarette, gauze covering the lower half of a face wrecked by cancer.

*

Survival guide:
1. Stop. Listen to the beating of your heart. Look out at the wild cherry trees laden with fruit.

*

The swallows have already built their nests above the back door; this is how, every year, H. notices the coming of spring. They are useful birds, and beautiful, and have always been a favorite of his. But now he watches them as he never has before, because he might not see another spring.

*

But what is frightening is not the thought of the unknown: it is the thought that there may not be an unknown, only an end.

*

In the village square, under what is now a small public garden there once stood a cemetery. It grew too small for so many deaths, so they built another. The dead remained where they were buried and in the new garden – a sort of communal grave – they placed a small stone plaque:

> *O ye who enter here,*
> *remember your*
> *forefathers, parents,*
> *grandparents, and friends*
> *who are buried here*

*

After many, many kilometers, the villages are all one.

*

She wakes up in the morning, has breakfast with her husband, sits to make lace, cooks lunch, then eats with her husband; in the afternoon, when she can, she rides down the hill in the tractor her husband drives, tends to her garden, and, when she can't, sits once again to make lace; she has dinner with her husband, talks to her children on the phone, watches a bit of tv, the lace in her lap.

On the living-room table lies a doily and on it a candlestick and a small statuette of three dolphins. The backs of the couches are also covered in lace.

Everything is clean, tidy. She smiles the whole time. Some would say a smile doesn't suit her. Even as her immaculate living room is filled with the sound of her colostomy bag, she smiles.

*

PALLIATIVE: 1. Serving to palliate. 2. A treatment that does not cure, but that assuages the illness. 3. Something to weaken the pain or postpone a crisis; postponement. 4. A disguise.

*

He's been bedridden for so many years that death is no longer a novelty. His skin is the thinnest white and, from his bed, he asks that the window always be left open. In the springtime, echoes of joy enter, and in the winter, snow. He has surrounded himself with saints to comfort him in sickness, as they previously had in poverty. Above the door, through which he will never walk again, is written:

> *God*
> *Grant me the serenity*
> *to accept the things*
> *I cannot change,*
>
> *The courage to change*
> *the things I can,*
> *And the wisdom to know*
> *the difference.*

*

AGONY: 1. Last struggle against death. 2. [Figurative] Anguish, affliction. 3. An imminent conclusion (preceded by a great disturbance).

'Agony,' the dictionary does not note, is a technical term.

*

On his first day of work, the nurse arrived at three in the afternoon and at four a patient died. He no longer knows how many deaths he has witnessed – on many nights he sleeps at the bedside of the dying – and yet he knows each death is different and that some are more difficult to manage than others. The hardest was that of a woman who, barely younger than his mother, had died of cancer. When he first started visiting her house, she could still cook for her children, who were not much younger than he was and had lost their father the previous year. When she stopped getting out of bed, the nurse started going there every day. He took care of her up until the moment they put her body in a coffin, and then he attended her funeral, where he laid his hands on the shoulders of her sons, who could have been his own brothers.

It was then that he made a pact with himself: every time a patient died, he would stop to think a moment. Now, when a patient dies, he sets aside at least fifteen minutes and asks himself: could I have done better?

*

Any resemblance between these characters and real people is no mere coincidence, and it is highly likely you know someone in the same situation.

*

Last year, it took an average of thirty-eight days for a person to die in their home, in those villages and small towns spread across an area of 1,728 square kilometers.

If you don't want to know the answer, don't ask the question.

*

The road, the road, the road, the road, the road, the road, the road, the road, the road, the road, the road, the road, the road . . . A bird of prey snatches her kill off the tarmac then flies away . . . The road, the road, the road, the road, the road, the road, the road, the road, the road, the road, the road, the road, the road, the roa

*

The hunter who liked flowers also liked collecting animals and displaying them above the living-room cabinet. The hunter who liked flowers also liked his wife to feel like his prey: frightened and cornered. He had been unhappy for most of his life in a city in another country; he had suffered humiliations, but he also liked to humiliate others. The last time, using only his eyes, he had made his wife feel as if *she* should be the one to die first. When he knew he would not survive his illness and that he would no longer be able to walk through the vast field in front of his house, the hunter who liked flowers begged for mercy, begged them to kill him quickly, please. He died in bed having said no meaningful last words and, that day, in the yard, a pup that would never grow up to be a hunting dog was born. The hunter was carried to a coffin and his wake was held in his living room – the stuffed birds with their fanned-out wings watching from their perch above the cabinet. The porch overlooks a view of the land that had been his greatest pride and that he had hoped to enjoy in his old age. On it stood his favorite flowerpot, in which flowers bloomed even in the spring after his death.

Whenever the wife of the hunter who liked flowers glances through the bedroom door, she sees her husband climb into bed, lie down, die. She sees him dying over and over and not once does he ask for her forgiveness. She still sleeps beneath his accusing eyes, and asks herself why, if it had indeed been her duty, she had not gone first. She lives alone now and the flowers he left behind are of little comfort to her.

*

An island, but instead of sea, land.

*

The swimming pool is empty. This somehow makes it seem bigger. The woman looks out at the pool from her window and thinks of the years that have passed since it was last filled with water and people – so many people, from so many villages (where have they all gone?) – and of how she would keep the bar open into the night, as long as there were customers to serve. From her window she sees the loneliness of the land. When she speaks to her neighbors, she yells to make sure she is heard. Her husband died deceived, blessedly deceived: he never knew what he suffered from, never knew he was condemned. She lied to him every day with conviction: it was the best way she knew of protecting him and she does not regret it. But she suspects that death begins long before we fall ill, with neither suffering, nor drama, nor a single memorable occurrence.

*

CONSPIRACY OF SILENCE: 1. Technical term used to describe a situation in which family members will conceal the patient's illness from the patient. The doctor is either persuaded to do so as well or will suggest maintaining the illusion. 2. Term also used in situations where the patient will pretend not to know what he or she knows about his or her illness and, thinking that their family members know nothing, will ask the doctor to conceal this information from the rest of the family. 3. In which the patient pretends not to know the gravity of the situation and pretends he or she doesn't know that the family knows.

*

As the sun sets over the plateau, white houses gleam momentarily then settle into darkness. Later, there will

23

be those who sleep while others do not. It is always worse at night, when the sick become agitated and their families wake up and spend the night fearing it might be the last. And if it isn't, in the morning they realize they do not feel relieved.

*

At the end of the road is a village from which the children have disappeared. And at the end of another road, another village from which the children have disappeared.

*

In the village there is a chapel, a communal oven, eight lived-in houses. There is no café, grocery, post office, town hall, or bus stop. On one side of the village, there is a hill that caught fire last summer, an event remembered not only for the alarm it caused, but also for its beauty. On the other side snakes a steep road that freezes in the winter and is often impassable. People here live their lives between their homes and their gardens, inhabitants of a Pompeii that has suffered no such natural disaster.

*

There are metaphors along the road: ripe fruit falling from trees; paths cut off abruptly; and the journey itself, an age-old metaphor for life and for the end of life. And yet, the surest metaphor for death is war: a person struggling in bed for years and years until their breathing is finally mistaken for moaning.

*

We obsess over lasts as we do over firsts. Last days, last images, last words. We want signs.

*

I knock on the door of a man who knows he will die, hoping he'll tell me how it feels to be a man who knows he will die. He has prepared his family for their mourning so that it is easier on them; he has said goodbye to those he wanted to say goodbye to.

The nurse shaves his beard so that he may appear dignified despite the pajamas, the diapers, the drool. For a few seconds, the man, his eyes bulging, looks at me, a stranger. His eyes roll back into his head. I haven't made it in time. The man can no longer speak. He is focused solely on dying, a task that seems to require a tremendous effort.

*

Survival Guide:
2. Think of death in detail. Don't think of the whole.

*

There are crosses on the way, marking car crashes. There are crosses on the way, marking people who fell off horses. There are crosses on the way, marking people who died while walking along its edge. The crosses are made of stone, some are very old and others ghostly new.

*

All that survived in the fire that began with an electric blanket and ended with a wrecked room was a Bible. This was considered a miracle, a sign that God is vigilant and watches over us despite all proof to the contrary. The woman who kept the Bible that survived the fire as a talisman lives with her widowed sister and with a niece who neither talks nor walks; who spends days on end in a windowless room; who, at fifty-seven, still cries and is easily startled; who is scared of strangers and for whom the world – she was very young when she once went to see a doctor in a neighboring country – is no more than those two or three streets.

God visits in the spring, and in the winter, perhaps having forgotten, He does not watch over her to see if she rolls her wheelchair into the light.

*

The same road does not seem the same, and yet every road seems the same. We move in circles, like eagles.

*

Up until just two months ago the shepherd, accompanied by his mad and lovesick wife, would walk every day to the São João fountain to drink water, striving for his miracle. Now he no longer leaves the back room of the retirement home; the room's windows look out onto the yard and have been blacked out with plastic. He lies shrunken in bed, with an oxygen tank by his side, in a blue robe the color of his eyes. That is where they hid him from his wife who, at the age of eighty, still insisted on trying to sleep with him, which is how he fell out of bed and ended up in the hospital. But his wife, who now sits in the waiting room, sometimes more and sometimes less absent than the rest of the home's elderly, has already forgotten him. She has forgotten she had a husband who she'd been madly in love with from the age of eighteen, and who made her violently jealous. She no longer asks about him and, when asked herself, answers she was never married. When he dies, she might not even realize and might not even cry.

Perhaps the shepherd, lying in bed with eyes closed, has flashes of his childhood raising sheep on the hill behind the home. At the top of the hill sit the ruins of a castle, proof of the village's former importance, proof that nothing important lasts.

On the hill there is a sculpture trail that re-enacts the Passion of Christ, and maybe that's why the shepherd believed there was something sacred in that spot where he would spend nights sleeping under the open sky.

In the same way that some will wait their whole lives to win the lottery, playing the same numbers over and over, week after week, the shepherd repeated the prayers his grandparents had taught him, hoping he might see the Virgin – as Francisco, Jacinta and Lúcia had in Fátima. He was intensely devoted to the three little shepherds and had visited the shrine there three times. He thought those kinds of miracles, real miracles, were the privilege – the only privilege – of the poor. After growing up and becoming a father, after growing old, and even up until just a few weeks ago, when his cancerous lung still allowed him to walk to the São João fountain to drink water, striving for his miracle, he would look towards the hilltop and it would seem to him that She was there. Watching.

*

And at night, in dreams, the old are young and the sick, healthy; in our minds we are no more than ourselves and in our dreams the best of ourselves.

*

The blinds on the upper floor are drawn, the tables and chairs wrapped in plastic. Her husband proudly shows off their large living room, as well as the other fully furnished rooms and their fully equipped bathroom. He built all this for his wife, even though she can no longer walk up the stairs and they are now both confined to two or three rooms on the ground floor.

*

Man is not God. Man is not God. Man is not God. Man is not God. Man is not God. Man is not God. Man is not God. Man is not God. Man is not God. Man is not God. Man is not God. Man is not God. Man is not God. Man is not God. Man is not

We should scrawl this in notebooks, filling page after page. We should be punished for thinking we can control everything, even death; for thinking that we can foresee it, and, who knows, maybe even avoid it.

*

The eagle soars in circles high above the river bluffs. Standing beside the water, with our feet planted on the earth, we are tiny; we are creatures governed by fear.

*

Survival Guide:
3. Make people into characters.
4. Don't stop crying over characters.

*

She wore black for years before she died because in the end it was her husband, who had fallen ill after her, also with cancer, who died first. She even lived to see her great-granddaughter baptized; it happened in August, the month of saints, promises, and celebrations. This was her first great-grandchild and her emigrant son had wanted the baby to be baptized in his parents' village. She'd had many children, but only the 'girl,' her handicapped daughter, was still with her. Before she died, they assured her that the 'girl,' by then thirty-nine years old, would be looked after at an institution. They came and took her. Her mother told her it wouldn't be for long.

And so, before she died, she found herself alone. She'd already stopped tending to her garden, then she stopped sitting at her front door, in the shade of her flowers, from where she used to like looking out at the other side of the street, at the house that belonged to her son who lived abroad – a large, freshly painted house. She would come to forget those she had recently met, but she never forgot any of her children, even those who had died as babies – on the fingers of one hand she counted the children she still had and on the fingers of the other the ones she had lost. It was strange that a body that was once so fertile could now be so barren. Before she died, she underwent so many operations that there was now nothing in her belly but the pains she felt like rocks in her gut. She was left with a scar that gave her the inhuman appearance of possessing two bellies, and she carried a bag for her needs. Not long before she died, she stopped getting up because when she did she would feel dizzy and fall and one day she even banged her head. She spent her days in bed in a room that was cool and dark in the summer, and cold and grim after it, and in which still stood the bed that had once belonged to the 'girl.'

*

O blessed Mother, who in your voyages have known weariness and the dangers of travel, protect these your children who are now embarking on a journey, be with them always, watch over their well-being and their needs, and help them arrive safely at their destination. Let it be so.

*

In the café they don't talk about people who are bedridden or in homes, of the old slowly vanishing. They talk about sudden and unexpected deaths, which are considered events. They talk, for example, about a boy who died just hours after he turned eighteen. He died on a distant foreign road, but was buried in his parents' village. The motorcycle he crashed was a birthday present. There was not a single visible scratch on his body, the café owner explained, so they held an open-casket wake.

*

Immortal in the morning. At night, the fear of never waking.

*

And yet another metaphor: the border. The eagle crossing it, circling. How easy it is to believe in the immortality of eagles.

*

I return to the first village. Daughter and granddaughter have gone back to the city and so the widow is now alone. She goes to the cemetery every day, where not only her husband but also her parents and siblings are buried. Her husband asked that, instead of a tombstone, a simple cross be placed over his grave, and she respected his request. Our Lady didn't heed the wish she made before he died – that she be taken three days after him, since she didn't want to be left behind – but she continues to pray, with discipline, and goes to church every day. She is not sure her husband can hear her but she prays that God will pass her message along.

The empty house seems to breathe. When she lies down, the iron bed she shared with her husband for over sixty years creaks loudly. In the dead of night, it is almost as if the figures in the framed black-and-white photographs that hang above the dresser were shifting.

Even though she's been afraid of being on her own ever since she heard about the burglars, she refuses to move to the city. She does not want to leave behind her village or her home, her bed and her photographs, the cherry orchard, her vegetable garden, the olive grove and chestnut trees, her ancient donkey, or her family's graves in the cemetery.

It is in her village and in her home that her husband lives on. For her, as well as for telephone companies:

'Hello?'

' . . . '

'He isn't home. He's in heaven.'

'. . .'

'Look, my daughter will be here tomorrow or the day after and can talk to you then.'

Her daughter always visits. An only child, she was always close to her parents. She looks like her mother, with a long face and a stoic air. On one of her visits, she brought along the book she was reading, *The Kite Runner*, and said the greatest gift her father, who was illiterate, had given her was the ability to read books like *The Kite Runner*, and to know where faraway cities like Kabul were. As she said this, she cried, even though the doctors had told her before her father died that she would no longer be able to produce tears.

*

In the cemetery: a photograph and at times no more than a name. Names may survive, but they were never what made us unique.

*

The photograph of the great-grandfather who traveled the world hangs on a wall in the hallway. In the picture stands an elegant man in a suit with an antique traveling bag and an old-fashioned mustache. The family walks through the hallway, carrying trays of food for the dinner party. They no longer glance at their great-grandfather. He is distant in the way someone whose voice you've never heard is distant. Pictures also die.

*

At the entrance to each village, right before or right after the exit off the main road, there is typically a Virgin. Normally, she is inside a bell jar, as if needing special care; as if, without the glass, and unprotected by people, she in turn would be incapable of protecting them.

*

The boy skates from one end of the empty café to the other, pretending not to hear the conversation taking place between his parents and the nurse. They are talking about medication, about nutrition, about how much longer his father will have to wait for a liver transplant. His mother speaks loudly, and briskly, having decided to spare her husband the need to discuss his own health. The boy's skateboard makes a monotonous sound on the café floor reminiscent of a fan or any machine that, when left on in an empty room, amplifies the silence. Out there runs a wide road, but there are few cars. A client comes into the café for coffee. The boy stops skating, goes to the counter, serves him; the man leaves again. Out there might lie a continent of wide-open spaces, yes, of large deserts. The boy resumes skating, resumes his role as just another teenager, pretending once again to feel alienated and unconcerned with the passing of time.

*

ILLUMINED: 1. One who cannot be dazzled. 2. One who is not blinded by too much light, and will not allow themselves to be enthralled. 3. One who sees the world lucidly, as equal parts pain and joy.

*

The nurses and social workers who work with the terminally ill have the look of those who have dedicated their lives to something larger than themselves (as it sometimes is with monks, who renounce their very identities), or of those who hold convictions they deem unshakable (as it sometimes is with Muslims). They do not seem cynical or guarded, as you might expect from those who live with death on a daily basis.

*

Land, roads, people, time, time, people, roads, land. What matters here is different, very different.

*

'Be quiet, or the doctor will take you to the hospital,' she says, and her husband stops groaning. He hasn't talked or walked for a year now and only eats when she threatens him with a trip to the hospital. What is it he sees as he lies in bed? Or does he simply keep his eyes closed and live in other images?

*

When our legs stop working, we will walk through our memories. When our legs stop working and our eyes stop seeing, we will walk through our memories and they will be clear. When our legs stop working, our eyes stop seeing and our ears stop hearing, we will walk through our memories and they will be clear, and forgotten voices will recount everything once more.

*

Articulated beds, diapers, morphine, gauze, creams for cuts and abrasions, serum drips, tubes, needles – illnesses come with practical problems that need solving; and death is chiefly a physical process. There is little that is literary about death.

*

On the road, '25 Minutes to Go' – Johnny Cash singing like a doomed man.

In any case, our lives are all on a timer, and it would be best not to forget it.

*

When the tour boat glides by, the river hides itself.

*

A. died. And so his family, finally free to lend a hand, came together. A. left behind a daughter he'd barely seen. She lived far away and would probably not make it in time for the funeral.

*

A GOOD DEATH: 1. A peaceful death, with minimal suffering. 2. A death in which both the dignity and identity of the dying are maintained up until the last moment. 3. A death in which the person dying is surrounded by family.

*

There's something of the missionary in the way the doctor makes her way by road, tracing circles, not only caring for the ill at each turn, but also spreading the word about the good death.

Hers is a big soul. Not like the strangler character in Miguel Torga's Trás-os-Montes story 'Alma Grande,' as terrifying as the very fear of death, but someone who will hold your hand as she chases away that fear.

The families are grateful, and years later will still tell her their news, as they would someone they'd shared a sacred moment with, as, for example, with a midwife.

*

There's a cross by the road. By the road, there's a cross.

*

Throughout the house are paintings, saints, flags from far-flung countries. She has never left the village. Her children traveled once they'd grown up. Her husband also traveled, spending most of their marriage abroad. He would only come home on holidays, and, even so, she never left him. He only came back for good once he'd grown old. He was out of his mind, yelling at her, threatening her. He can no longer remember this, but his eyes are still full of rage and the desire to harm. He has stopped eating, which is perhaps another way of hurting her. Or perhaps, in his dementia, he knows she has more than enough reason to poison him. Maybe he doesn't think any of this; the bad man has simply lost his appetite.

*

On bedside tables, clocks mark the times for their medications. No one seems to notice the irony in having clocks at the bedsides of the dying.

*

In the country she emigrated to, they say people go to heaven. At home, as a child, she would hear them say: he's dead, and he won't be coming back. She chooses to come die at home.

*

Man has blood on his hands, but God has more. Man has the dead on his mind, but God does, too. Man has nightmares, but God does not sleep.

*

Fear in the eyes of the man who will not walk. He fears falling. He fears staying fallen and looking up from all the way down there, at the books he can no longer read, on their tall shelves; or falling in the yard, lying on the cold ground and looking up at the tips of fruit trees and at birds hopping towards his eyes. He thinks his wife wouldn't be able to lift him; that she would have to call for help and that others would see him, fallen; that they would have to then pick him up and wipe the bird droppings off, or, if he was in the house, drag him towards the sofa, which was actually so very near. As he pictures this, he shakes even more. He stops talking to keep from shaking. He stops thinking to keep from shaking. Later, he will come to forget the word Parkinson's.

*

. . . pray for us sinners, now and at the hour of our death. Amen.

*

The little boy rides his bike down a carless street that seems very long to him. At the end of one street is another, and then the field: the world in all its possibility and impossibility. When he returns to his village many years from now, if there is still a village, he will see how small that street really was, and the field, just a little larger than a backyard. Perhaps, many years from now, he won't see any children drawing their whole wide worlds and he will feel like an endangered species.

*

Now and at the hour of our death.

*

During the last week of his life, she thought every night would be his last; that the following day, she would no longer hear her husband breathing. After a while, she was so tired she started hoping it would happen quickly. Then she would feel guilty and start crying because he had not eaten his yogurt at breakfast.

*

Now.

*

The last notes I take are about a man who sings to his wife. After she was diagnosed with leukemia, he began to play the guitar again. When she came home from the hospital one year ago, M. thought she would die soon after. But she got better once she was home, and so they began their second life together.

'*Todos me querem eu quero algum / quero o meu amor / não quero mais nenhum.*' He played and sang as she tapped her feet and hummed along from the living-room sofa because, even though her memory sometimes failed her, she could still remember the melodies. Whenever he played on local radio stations, he dedicated every song to her.

They never had kids. When they got married, she was already nearing the age when women no longer have children. Being so much younger than she was, he must have known that one day he would end up taking care of her, but perhaps he had never realized how difficult it would be. He is all she has.

In these last notes, M., weak after spinal surgery, no longer plays the guitar. He now lives each day with the fear that something might happen to him and that she will then be left alone. But he doesn't say this. He says he promised Our Lady a hundred euros – he saw Her over the door to the operating theater – and that the operation had gone well, so now everything could go back to being as normal, as alive, and as musical as ever. M. plays a recording of his own voice on an old hand-held recorder so that he does not have to speak.

*

And even if words survive, they'll be too old to comprehend.

*

The girl walks down the steps, slowly, her legs like a ragdoll's, with one hand held up to her chest. She leaves the house, slowly, and comes outside to sit on the bench in the sun with the old women.

*

Survival Guide:
5. Shadow the circling eagles. Imagine their nests.

*

Where is Ivan Ilyich? Where is the agony Tolstoy wrote? Where are the men who look back at the moment they became men? Where are regret and forgiveness? And the fulfillment, if there was any, felt in those joyful years? The sick suffer, and then have no strength left to think or to ask themselves those moral questions – nor do they even seem concerned (is this unique to our time?) with heaven, hell, or the Last Judgment. They just want a little more life, they want just a little more time to believe that the body can triumph; everyone wants, with disproportionate and perhaps delirious intensity, to carry on living.

*

And then love, the great survivor of all disaster.

*

If I were to go back there and knock on the door once more, and then again and again; if I had time, unhurried time, and pretended I wasn't born in the city; if I knew how to listen more carefully, every word acknowledged and cared for; if I knew what to do with my hands and how not to take notes: would people open up and tell me what they really think about in those slow and lonely nighttime hours?

*

And finally, hands writing against hoarded images.

*

Grass as tall as children, on the roadside, dancing. In the horizon, hills meeting like lovers. All this in the deepest purple, seconds after the sun sets.

PORTRAITS

Though wise men at their end know dark is right,
Because their words had forked no lightning they
Do not go gentle into that good night.

DYLAN THOMAS
'Do Not Go Gentle into that Good Night'

Our almost-instinct almost true:
What will survive of us is love.

PHILIP LARKIN
'An Arundel Tomb'

PAULA

It's August and the smell of fireworks is in the air. Somewhere, the band that will play at the dance is doing a soundcheck.

At the kitchen table, Paula takes a handful of her daughter's hair, straightens it with a straightening iron, rests it on her daughter's shoulder, and then picks up another. She takes her time, and these are the only gestures I see her make that aren't impatient.

Twelve-year-old Ana has painted her nails and her eyes are made up beneath her thick brown eyebrows. The only childlike thing about her is her Hello Kitty watch. She wears a top just like her mother's, with a wide neckline and metallic detail on the shoulder. She wears beige, her mother blue. Arm in arm, they walk down the street.

But, no, it wasn't like that. I'm getting mixed up. It wasn't on the night of the dance that you could smell fireworks, but the next day, when the family gathered for lunch, and there were all kinds of meat roasting

49

over a wood fire from eight in the morning, and potatoes seasoned with savory and fresh thyme. In the closed café, the small tables had been pushed to the side and replaced with a larger one covered in a white, embroidered cloth. The family gathered inside the cool, dark café at the hottest time of day, when the light is blinding: mother, stepfather, the aunt who lived in Porto, the firefighter brother, and the emigrant brother who had traveled from Belgium. Ana was as busy as the older women, carrying trays from one side of the street to the other, from the house to the café. Luís, the youngest, barely ate. He was distracted, his eyes glued to the television and his thoughts somewhere far away, in America.

And then, looking back again, this lunch could easily be another, held two months later, on the day they harvested the grapes from Paula's vineyard: Casimiro, her husband, grabbing beers from the freezer; the men and women who worked the harvest still drinking, as they had all morning, under the sun, which beat down mercilessly despite the calendar claiming fall had arrived. They spoke of the longevity of trees. They spoke of the long list of medicines taken by their respective husbands and wives who would not live as long as the trees. At that lunch, Paula barely ate; she'd recently been to the dentist – the culmination of a series of tooth extractions required by her chemotherapy – and the anesthetic made her nauseous. She seemed even more irritable at that lunch than at the one in

August, when her husband, children, and siblings had all been around and she'd had no time for herself, and had focused every minute on being alive.

Then there was the lunch by the river, after a fishing contest, where we ate bean stew, and the money collected for food and drink was set aside for the festival thrown in August in honor of Our Lady of Good Health, the village's patron saint. It was June, and hot for spring. Paula wore a sun hat and spoke of the river and of village life. It was only when she became annoyed with her youngest son, who kept running about too close to the water, or with her husband, because of some harmless gesture he made, that the effort in her happiness became noticeable.

That was the day Paula introduced me to her husband and children, the day she showed me the family café, open now only to friends, and the village. Peredo da Bemposta was at the end of a very long road – a good twenty minutes from the highway that connects Mogadouro to Miranda do Douro – and it was on the drive home from Peredo that I realized it is impossible to travel to the end of the world without wanting to go back there. I would want to go back over and over because time and again I would want to recover what, in my world (the center?), seemed to have been lost: a certain way of demonstrating love.

That Sunday went by quickly. Before I returned to Miranda do Douro, we stopped at Algosinho, the village next to Peredo, where Casimiro was born. We stopped there to visit a church that is a kind of stone palimpsest: the Star of David beneath the Cross of Christ.

Nearby stand the graves the villagers claim date from the time of the Moors, sculpted in the shape of the bodies underneath: two graves side by side – for a couple – and a smaller grave a few feet away, the size of a child no more than two years old. It was strange being there with that family, contemplating the graves of another family from another, distant century like they would any other monument, as if death were just a spectacle, something that happens to other people – or rather, something very ancient.

I left with the sunset in the rear-view mirror, as Paula and her family drove away in another car along another road. I think it was on that day, or perhaps the next, when, unable to stop thinking of that couple's grave, I decided to patch things up with my partner.

I went back there in the autumn, on the day of Paula and Casimiro's grape harvest, around seven in the morning, and I parked the car next to the church with the Star of David. There was nothing but the sound of dogs barking and a few birds singing. I was alone, and yet I was never alone anymore now that there was another life growing inside me. I watched the sunrise throw the land into light, a daily, perhaps even trivial, sight, but one that just then seemed to me unique. This is what we humans are like. After watching the universe materialize as if I were the only person in the world, I fell asleep, and then woke up again, the sun high and the harvested grapes in their baskets.

But it is in August that Paula attends the procession. Her daughter, dressed for the occasion, follows her at a distance, almost as if watching over her, one hand holding on to one of the purple ribbons attached to the figure of Christ being carried solemnly along the village streets. Her husband, in his Sunday best, follows the procession from afar, smoking heavily. From the windows, beautiful bright drapes and immaculate white curtains stream down the walls. The priest's voice echoes through the loudspeakers and the village, preaching that parents must look after their children so that later on their children might look after them. 'God be with us. Amen.'

Paula walks barefoot over the hot and dusty August street. She has delicate feet, long and thin, and her toenails are painted. The procession continues up the last street and ends at the small chapel by the graveyard with the best view in the village: seen from here, the land seems to run on like time itself.

In the chapel there is only enough room for the Christ figure and for a couple of benches, where Paula now sits. Ana kneels down and helps her mother put on her shoes. They don't speak. Their eyes aren't wet with tears. Their expressions don't change.

And it was there, by the chapel, when the procession was finished and the vows made, that the men launched the fireworks, painting the clear August sky with fleeting clouds that concealed small, contented, finite gods.

The dance, then, had actually been the night before the procession, the night before hope. The lights that bounced off the stage swept the tarmac while the younger children chased the white, red, and blue spots. The speakers, distorting the music, made even our bones quiver, and the singer changed her costume as often as if she were in a 1950s vaudeville show.

Mother and daughter danced in their identical tops without looking each other in the eyes. They twirled around one another, neither shy nor brazen. They danced as if they spent every night on a dance floor, as if each knew with absolute certainty that she would hold the other in her arms forever. As if it weren't August and as if August, especially this August, weren't flying by far too quickly.

Later, August had come and gone. Paula seemed thinner in the face, wearier, yet also more serene. In their house in the town, Mogadouro, where the family spends the school year, Ana did her homework in her room, decorated on one side with Hello Kittys and on the other, Luís's side, with Spidermen. Paula, alone in the living room, the tv on in the background, did not wrinkle her nose, nor were there creases around her closed mouth. Her face, now relaxed, revealed how wounded she was.

I thought of the bullfights at the festival in Trás-os-Montes in August, of how the bulls fought, of how the more they suffered, the fiercer they were, wowing the crowd with their apparent invincibility – dying in the arena they are, at least briefly, immortal.

Whenever I try to remember Paula's face, I see it as it was in August, with the obstinate expression of one who refuses to accept defeat. Even now, when I think of her, I always think of August and I believe I'll think of her every August, and of her village, beating like a fragile heart.

Night is falling by the time Luís comes home from school. He scatters his notebooks on the living-room table and shows his grades to his mother, who scolds him for his poor marks. Not long after, Casimiro comes home from work. Ana, who is still doing her homework in her room, doesn't come down. Casimiro takes a beer from the fridge. Paula sets the table and finds something to talk about, as if for her the day had been very eventful. Whenever there's a lull in the conversation, Paula glances at the muted television and Casimiro lowers his eyes to his beer. They can hear the ticking of the wall clock painted with two skyscrapers lit up in the night.

this summer I let everything go: I spent time with my family – with my husband and my kids – and I didn't feel a thing, I mean, sure, sometimes I'd be in a bit of pain, so I'd take something, 'cause the pain was in my bones, and your body can feel the lack of chemo, but I just gritted my teeth, and even then . . . it was like there was nothing wrong with me, and now it's hard to start the chemo again, but if that's what I've gotta do . . . 'cause they can't make any guarantees, even if you do get your treatment it's still there inside you, they can't guarantee it won't come back, but it's something, I guess. It's like everyone says, if you do the chemo then even if it does come back, it won't be as bad, but if you don't get any treatment at all, it might come galloping back even harder

life changes completely from one day to the next, and that's when you realize that there's no use fighting wars, there's no use getting annoyed – life's too short – and it changed my way of thinking, my way of being . . . now I live more for my children, I pay closer attention to what people tell me, everything's different now, I try to make the most of things, to have more fun, and, sure, I used to be more cheerful, but back then I had my whole life ahead of me . . . not anymore though, now I know I'm sick, I know I might have another two or three years left, or maybe just a few months, and so I'm trying to take life one day at a time, I'm trying to give the best of myself to my husband, to my children, 'cause I want to make my kids as happy as I can, for as long as I can

I don't like sitting still, I want to be out doing things and I know I can't, it's so frustrating . . . we used to own this café in the village, it was my mom's, but then we had to close it . . . I met my husband at that café . . . She bought it when I was eighteen years old and that's where we met and where we started dating, we dated for a whole six years before we got married, I was twenty-four and he was twenty-six . . . I'd had boyfriends before, I wasn't the sort to just watch life go by, and I dated this one boy my mom really liked . . . me and my husband, we dated in secret – our moms didn't want us seeing each other so that's why we dated for so long, although then we broke up and I got back together with the other guy for a bit, but finally I ended up with Casimiro . . . that other boy really liked me – he liked me so much that even when I was handing out wedding invitations, he went and he talked to my mom and he told her not to let me get married 'cause he was the one I was supposed to marry . . . he's in Lisbon now, he's a police officer, and I guess love really is blind, because he was richer, but I was in love with Casimiro, so what could I do? We were married for three years before we had children, we'd go to all these parties, I had all the fun I'd missed out on when I was single, then Ana was born and we didn't have Luís until five years later, 'cause we had all the time in the world, we had all the time in the world ahead of us and we weren't in a hurry to do anything at all

it was an adventure, it really was – I was sixteen, and four of us girls went away to Macau, one of them was my husband's sister, but I didn't know my husband back then, I'd only seen him around . . . they wanted to open a restaurant out there and this cousin of mine, who was a priest in Macau, he said he'd get hold of four girls from here to take over there – I didn't even think twice about it, all I wanted was to go and my mom let me, so I went . . . I really liked Macau, it's somewhere I'd go back to, it's a seventeen-hour trip so we stopped in Frankfurt to switch planes and we couldn't really speak the language, we didn't know anything at all, but luckily we met this woman who was going to Macau too, to meet her husband who was a vet over there, and she helped us get there, that's the kind of adventure it was . . . later that woman moved from Macau to Porto, and when I was sick I found out she was a volunteer at the oncology hospital in Porto, she pushes the tea cart . . . we go years without seeing each other and then that's where we end up meeting . . . in Hong Kong we took a boat to Macau and the four of us shared an apartment there, but then the restaurant didn't work out . . . it was so great out there, though, I can't even describe it, I loved everything about it – that's where I tried Chinese food for the first time, and we traveled, the priest took us traveling to China, to Thailand – in Thailand, we visited this really tall hotel that had this area where you could sit at a table and just watch, and then, after a little while, you were suddenly looking at something else, another view, it was great, really great, even though the Chinese were dirt poor, it wasn't as bad in Macau – they ate rice with every meal there and sometimes I ate with them, but I used a knife and fork . . . I was sorry to leave, but I had to . . . I missed home, sure, but when you're that age you barely feel it, you just want to go out all the time and that's it. Those days, talking on the phone was a luxury, so we'd write lots of letters and send photos, I have a lot of photos from back then . . . I wish I'd traveled more, but who's got the money? Nobody we knew had the money for that kind of thing

my stepdad is like a father to me, his first wife died of the same thing I have and I think he's hurting as if he was my own dad . . . when he was sick just now, when he was in a coma, they told me I could go see him and so I did and when I sat next to him, it was . . . because we're real close it was disturbing to see him like that . . . the nurse asked if I was ok and I said, sure I am, except then I started crying, I said I am, but I won't come see him again while he's like this and she said, but you can hold his hand, you can talk to him, so I held his hand and I talked to him, but he didn't react, he just lay there . . . when he woke up from his coma and came home he told me what I'd said: so, honey, I guess you didn't want to see me, he said, and I said, what do you mean I didn't want to see you? I did want to see you and I went and I saw you . . . then he said, the first time you visited you told the nurse, I won't come see him again while he's like this, and you started crying . . .

59

and I asked, oh, who told you, and he said no one told me, I heard it, like I heard it when you were holding my hand and you said Claudino, Claudino don't leave me, I've already lost one father, I can't lose another

I lost my dad seventeen years ago, I'm forty now so I would've been twenty-three then, he died very suddenly – a heart attack – it was totally unexpected, he'd never been sick, he'd always been so healthy, but one day when he was getting out of bed, he just keeled over and that was it

I had the operation on July 23, 2008, I was thirty-seven years old . . . my son was turning four on July 28 and I was in the hospital, the poor boy . . . my kids, they wanted to come see me in the hospital, and I wanted to see them, too, but I was plugged into a serum drip and into all these machines and I asked them to take it all out, so that at least they wouldn't have to see me like that, plugged in, and the nurses took it all out, and the kids came, and their mom was lying in bed and she couldn't move, but at least they didn't have to see all those machines plugged into me

they only found the tumor when I was on the operating table . . . I'd been admitted to the hospital for a minor appendix operation, I was in a lot of pain, but they thought it was my appendix, and the doctor said, it's a minor operation – so minor I woke up in the middle of it and they had to give me more anesthetic and the whole thing lasted six hours . . . I had it done in Bragança, and the doctor who operated on me died two days later, something about a plane crash and the doctor just disappeared – they never found the body, it was all anyone talked about back then . . . they even said that the doctor had planned it himself 'cause he'd been having some personal problems and he'd wanted to disappear, and they never did find the body . . . he was the one who had started operating on me first, but then, when he found more than he'd bargained for he called in someone else 'cause he couldn't do it all on his own, and when he was explaining what was going on to the other doctor, this Spanish doctor, that's when I woke up, and I heard him telling him how it was supposed to be a minor appendix operation, but it was more complicated now, he said, she's got a tumor, and the tumor's been punctured, we've got a lot of work to do, but then maybe I moved, I'm not sure, I just know that he said, quick, quick the patient's waking up, the anesthetic's wearing off, we've got to give her more, but make it a stronger dose this time 'cause it's more complicated now and I don't know how long we'll be operating for . . . and I heard everything . . . I think those must have been the worst days of my life . . . when I got out of surgery, my son's godmother was there with one of my friends, they were both there and the doctor said he could only talk to family members, and they said, look, her husband is with the kids, but we're here on his behalf, we'd like to know, and the doctor told them. He told them what was happening, but they didn't tell me, instead my son's godmother told me, everything's ok, Paula, and I said, don't tell me everything's ok 'cause I know it's not, I know what's up, and she started crying, and I said, you don't have to lie to me, I know what's going on, and she just stood there with her mouth open, 'cause how could I know what was going on if I'd just got out of surgery? The day after the operation, the doctor came to talk to me and I said to him, tell me everything, don't try hiding anything from me, 'cause I heard you, and he said, we still don't know if the tumor's malignant or if it's benign . . . then they put me in the isolation ward, I was there for five days, and I wasn't allowed any visitors, they only let me see my husband and the priest – the one who took us to Macau – and my brother, the firefighter, he came in his uniform, but apart from them I didn't see anyone . . . when they let me out of isolation I was taken to a room and some nurses came with some paperwork from the oncology hospital, and they had a lot of questions for me and that's when it really hit me, 'cause when you see the word oncology you picture it all, you imagine the worst-case scenario, all kinds of things go through your head . . . when they got the results, the doctor, the Spanish one, he came and told me that they had the test results, but that it was treatable, he tried to make things sound less bad: it's treatable, he said, I got everything out, everything's clean, I didn't leave any of it in there, and . . . everything was clean in my intestines, but it'd already reached my liver by then . . . when you hear something like that, you think all kinds of things . . . why me? What did I do? You think . . . before this kind of thing happens, you think it's something that happens to other people, but never to you – it's something that happens to so-and-so, to someone else, but not to you, nothing's ever supposed to happen to you

this kind of thing is just so terrible that maybe it's better not to talk about it at all . . . I don't mind if other people do, but I try not to . . . when people ask me if I'm doing better now I say I'm fine, I always say I'm doing just fine, even though sometimes I'm not feeling all that great . . . and people say you don't even look sick, look at your complexion, you look really good, and I say, I'm not sick, I'm not sick at all, 'cause if you start saying you're sick, I think it's even worse then, you feel worse, and your friends, even your closest friends, they feel worse too – if there's anything we can do to help, anything at all, they'll say . . . and then it's harder for whoever's around, so it's better to always say you're ok, sometimes you might not be doing that great, but you still say you're doing just fine

I've got used to the idea of having this illness and it's just something I've got to deal with, it's not like it's going away . . . in the beginning, when it was only in my intestines, all I wanted was for it to go away, but then it reached my liver and that was it, the doctor told me the cancer had metastasized in my liver and it was there to stay . . . they explained that it was gonna keep growing, even if they cut it out, it would just keep growing . . . I was hoping they'd cut the root of it outta my liver and that that would be the end of it, but that's not what happened, so I had to get used to living with it, for however long I had left . . . I'd have to live with it and that was that. I got used to it, I've gotta get used to it

we go to bed, I wait for my husband to fall asleep, and then I get up and I walk downstairs, especially when I have an appointment the next day, and all kinds of things go through my head, everything, absolutely everything . . . what if something happens,

*what are we gonna do about the kids? When I'm down here on
my own, I think of them, of how they'll manage if I'm not here*

*sometimes, you think you can't do it, that you can't take it,
but then somehow or other you find the strength to keep going*

*we have to have faith and strength and we have to carry on
and that's what we're gonna do*

you only know what it's like when it happens to you

———————

Paula still managed to go to the festival in August 2012. Even in her
weakened state, with help from the team of palliative home-care
nurses, she attended the procession. She wanted to say goodbye to
all her friends. She died at home, surrounded by her family, at the
beginning of September 2012.

JOÃO AND MARIA

He pulls down his light, well-ironed shirt over his urine bag. He flicks his hat up, uncovering his eyes. He smiles. Finishes the card game. Wins. Smiles. He gets up and pays for the bottle of water. Says see you tomorrow. Smiles. He leaves the café. With his slim legs and slight swagger, he has the grace of vast landscapes. He pushes open the small gate that leads to his front yard, climbs the step to the porch and sits on a bench facing west, like in an old cowboy movie, the evening sun falling across his face. He smiles.

The woman walks out of the house, slowly, her legs swollen. She has tended to her garden and left everything ready in the kitchen so she can start cooking dinner later. She adjusts her headband on her graying hair and sits beside her husband. She doesn't lean back, but instead rests her hands on her knees, as if poised to get up again at any moment.

They greet the passers-by. They wait. Usually, nothing special happens. They wait. Together, they watch the sun set. The next day will be like this one, which has been just like the previous one.

Nearly every time I visited Santulhão, I'd found Senhor João and Senhora Maria sitting on their front porch. Except for the first time, when they'd been in their house. A folder containing the paperwork for the farm they had once owned in Angola lay on the kitchen table, beside boxes of medicines, as if placed there by chance. Inside was a document that read: 'Angola, Huíla province, 1965, João Manuel Fernandes, 35 years old, Originally from Santulhão, Farmer by trade, is hereby certified, having paid 300 escudos for this license, Hoque, Municipality or District of Lubango.' And from that moment on, in my mind Santulhão became linked to Angola.

I returned time and again to Santulhão. I was intrigued by Senhor João, a man who had clearly been a hypochondriac his whole life and who now had a very real and serious illness, cancer, but who smiled as he spoke melodramatically of how he suffered, of how little time he believed he had left.

Every time I went back there, I wanted to ask Senhor João if he was afraid of dying. I wanted to ask him what it was like to be eighty years old, what it was like to reach the end of your life: if he had any regrets, if it had all been worthwhile, and, if so, what exactly had been worthwhile? But instead I always ended up asking him about Angola, about how they had made it from there, Santulhão, in the Municipality of Vimioso, in Trás-os-Montes, to Hoque, Lubango, in the Huíla Province, in Angola; when, and why? How had they come back, how had they readjusted, and what place did those particular memories occupy in their minds?

They were rusty when it came to talking about their memories and about themselves. Like many from Trás-os-Montes, Senhor João and Senhora Maria would sometimes use third-person verb tenses when speaking in the first person. Instead of 'I have done' they would say 'I has done,' which gave the impression their lives could have been lived by someone else. Their story may not have been unique, but it was long. It would have to be reassembled with some perseverance, with a willingness to merge certain decades into others and with particular attention to sowing and to harvesting, to rain and to drought. Their story, to be honest, was never complete. Last time I visited, we spoke for so long that I ended up watching the sun set with them. I didn't know what so many hours of recorded material might be worth, but I thought of how my own grandfather always said that history is written by the rich, and I wanted to give Senhor João and Senhora Maria a right to theirs. And anyway, what sense does it make at the age of eighty to speak of death without speaking of everything you have lived? It would be like visiting your hometown without setting foot in your house.

It was clear, and did not have to be discussed at length, that their greatest fear was not death – that was for the young – but being left alone. Beyond that, it terrified them that they might lose their senses, and with them their memories, and with their memories the story of their lives. They don't want – Senhor João repeats, still smiling – to die in poor health. Because you could end up spending years lying in a bed or, if you're unlucky, in a bed in a home, or worse still, in a hospital bed, hooked up to machines and to tubes. Was it just their impression, or did people use to be healthier when they died?

When I visited them in August, illness was not their only company. The porch was no longer still, with children and grandchildren constantly coming in and out of the house. Their eldest son, who has since spent time in Angola trying to reclaim his parents' farm, and the emigrant son, who lives in France and who, that year, was a *mordomo* – one of the organizers of the August festival – were both in Santulhão. Their granddaughters, skinny little things from the city in skin-tight clothes, would get up late, wander to the kitchen and pick at the food left in their grandmother's pots and pans, their eyes feverish with both the doubts and the certainties of their futures. The grandchildren, more grown-up and more nostalgic by the year, wanted to talk about their childhood: about how they ran through fields, falling into ponds, then laughing into the night so they could stay awake and stretch out those long Trás-os-Montes summers.

In the house that belonged to their daughter-in-law, the wife of their eldest son, there was a large yard that had once been a corral. There, they barbecued Mirandesa steak and lean cuts, and the table was very long so everyone, family and friends, could fit around it. Senhor João and Senhora Maria ate calmly and spoke little. No one asked them much, but this didn't seem to bother them. On the contrary, they enjoyed listening to the loud muddled voices and observing the youthfulness that surrounded them, the spectacle of the different generations. At dinner they talked about the festival and about money, of which there was less and less for performances that were increasingly sophisticated; they talked about emigration: France, Angola, Brazil, the United States, Canada. After the meal, Senhor João and Senhora Maria did not go see the band play since the music would only begin after midnight, which was too late for them. Later, though only the faintest of sounds reached the porch, they could still feel the night's euphoria in their chests.

One time, after visiting Santulhão and hearing Senhor João talk about the dreams he'd had in which he returned to Angola, to farming and to hunting, I also dreamt of Angola. I went back there with my father and brother, we walked along a beach, and in my dream I was aware we were only visiting; we would soon leave. When I woke up the next morning, I couldn't stop thinking of the trip I'd taken to Luanda, years earlier, without my family. The cemetery, perched above the city, had impressed me. As I read the names on the tombstones a mother's voice cried out in the background, and I thought of how lucky we were that no one in our family had stayed behind, that none of us were buried there. 'Mommy has to leave you now, my love. Mommy has to go.' And as two men dragged the woman out of the cemetery, carrying her out in their arms, I finally understood how tragic it is to leave the dead behind, to leave them alone.

Now that their children have started traveling back to Angola, to try to reclaim the farm that was once theirs, in the south of the country, I wonder if Senhor João and Senhora Maria ever think of the possibility of their children moving so very far away, and then of their grandchildren leaving too; of how, after they die, the younger generations might never visit Santulhão again. The cemetery, which is just there, you can see it from their porch, to the left of the house and in front of the café – will it become a place exclusively for the dead?

It doesn't make Senhor João and Senhora Maria unhappy to spend their old age in the place they were born, and yet they can't but help feel that they've lost part of their identity to history and that there is more defeat in life than there ever will be in death.

Senhor João crosses his long, tanned hands over his belly, his urine bag pushed to one side, and turns to face the sun, the west, looking out into the distance. Senhora Maria looks out at her vegetable garden in their front yard, at the road, at her husband.

As they sit on the porch, at the end of the day, Senhor João and Senhora Maria see what the younger generations do not: bygone landscapes. In their eyes, the sun slowly bruising through long months of unbearable heat, there is still time to hope everything ends there, on that purple horizon.

HIM: *I dream more than I sleep. Or maybe it's all jumbled up. I don't know.*

HER: *Sure he dreams, and sometimes he kicks me, too. I ask him what's wrong and he says: oh, I was just hunting in Angola.*

HIM: *In Angola, we'd go hunting every week, sometimes even two, three times. There was wild goats, antelopes, game. Soon's the dry season hit, they'd come searching for drinking water.*

HER: *Goats, they'd come in bean season. One day he asked me: what we got for lunch tomorrow? 'Cause we had so many chickens and pigs and —*

HIM: *One year we killed eighteen of them!*

HER: *He said: look, there's a goat eating the beans. Gonna see if I can grab him. I hadn't even finished washing the dishes and there he was bringing in two of them goats. The blacks, they knew the sound of his gun and so they'd come knocking at my door the next day, saying I'm here to help with the skinning, Senhora. And I'd say, alright then, cut here and cut there and take this here for you.*

They'd be so darn happy! Senhora, you give us balela *today?*

HIM: *They called meat* balela.

HIM: *I'm eighty now. And here I am, fearful I might fall sick before I die. My kids, they tell me: you gotta try taking it one day at a time now.*

When I got back from Angola and had this operation in Vimioso, the doctor said to me: oh, you'll live to see eighty yet! But I felt downright bad. I don't know if it was because of how I had to leave Angola that I felt so bad, but I asked him, me, eighty? And now I've made it to eighty, you know what I'm hoping for? To make it to ninety. You know what makes me really happy? It's not doing the living myself, it's getting to see the family, the kids, the grandkids. My oldest grandson, he's a mechanical engineer, another one's studying to be an architect. The daughter of our eldest, she's a nurse. Another granddaughter, she's finishing up school to be a scientist. And she's already making a living at a university in France . . .

HER: *She's doing her PhD.*

HIM: *And my youngest son's kid, he's a police officer. I got no great-grandchildren yet. That's why a person's got to keep going.*

HER: *Our oldest grandkid is twenty-six, but he ain't given any thought to marriage yet.*

HIM: *It ain't easy living in the city. Here, in the village, we've got a house, a vegetable patch, and we just keep on.*

HER: *There ain't a day goes by we don't eat what our garden grows.*

HIM: *And then there's even some left for the kids.*

HER: *Folk don't go hungry here. Everyone's growing things. There's always enough.*

HIM: *But back in the day, the houses was full of people. Now everywhere's empty. There's some's left, others died. There's only five, six kids in the school now and they go to Vimioso, 'cause there ain't no schools in Santulhão anymore.*

HER: *Back then, families were big, they'd have ten, twelve kids, and you needed a plentiful garden to fill the pot. Folks went hungry. There was lice, and there were ticks. We were dirt poor back then.*

HIM [pointing at the houses opposite]: *Over there, where them houses are now, there was mud. And you mixed it in with straw and you had yourself some fertilizer.*

HER: *My ma was real sick, and truly devoted to the saints. She went down to Mirandela one time to pray, and me and my brother, we went with her and we saw this bicycle. We just stared at it, 'cause we'd never seen one before. No one bought us kids bikes, there wasn't any money for presents.*

HIM: *When I was about ten, we had a pair of stilts . . .*

HER: *They used to get all banged up.*

HIM: *. . . and we'd strap our feet into them and walk all over the place.*

HER: *We had seven kids. The first two died: one at five and a half months, the other when he was born. I cried and cried thinking that maybe none might survive . . . The best thing in life's your kids. Everything else is just . . . We left everything we had behind in Angola. But our kids, thank the Lord, they make enough to keep themselves afloat. They're smart and they've got skills enough to work. There never was much, but we sent them to school with the little we had.*

HIM: *There ain't a thing I regret selling.*

HER: *I would've sold our land so the kids could go to school. If we'd gone to school ourselves, we wouldn't've held onto our land like we did, we would've got jobs. He had to finish elementary school to get his driver's license in Angola.*

HIM: *Who finished elementary school round here back then? We worked like slaves.*

HIM: *When I went to Angola, there was lots of folks here and almost nowhere to harvest grain. Before that, I even tried getting to France. I gave a doctor from Bragança one and a half contos (speaking in contos, which is what we used back then). The doctor said he got people across the border and he had this middleman in Vimioso. The plan was that after he got me papers, I'd give him another one and a half contos. But time passed, and then some more . . . He must've conned 'bout six hundred people. There was lots of us waiting to go to France. And then in the end not one of us did. Those days, there wasn't any tv, but I heard this broadcaster say on the radio: come to Angola, my brothers, hardworking men of Trás-os-Montes. I had a cousin of mine in Angola and he was a sergeant in the army, and I wrote him a letter and then he wrote me back saying: cousin, you're not going to believe it! They harvest twice a year out here! First, two guys from over here went there, then me, then three more. Then it was like a flood: more than thirty folk from here went over.*

I was already sick back then. I'd say to her, I got an ulcer and she'd go, there ain't nothing wrong with you. I'd say, yeah there is, and I need surgery. Those days, you need an operation, you gotta pay, and we didn't have no money for that, we would've had to sell all we had, and that's why I left here so fast. But there in Luanda, with that food and that weather, I hurt even more. I was lucky enough, though, 'cause I knew someone there, a lady who was the daughter of a teacher from over here, the one who'd taught me my letters, and she was a teacher, too, and married to an engineer who was in charge of the railways, and he told me to go see his friend, who worked at a clinic. He wrote a little something on a piece of paper for me to show him and they saw me right then and there. They operated and then after the operation they told me: you gotta go on a diet now. But I was never much a nagger, I never asked for nothing. I was staying in this shelter and there was six hundred and some more of us there – there was family men, sick folk, some missing a hand, others who was blind. That was where all us outcasts went. All the poor folk were there and we lived crammed into this barrack made of zinc, it went from over here to about there, to that cherry tree. The outhouse was over a cesspit, there was just a lone plank of wood and no water. There was loads of old folk, some from here, some from Angola, folk who should've been in a home, and they were almost always fighting like dogs. When I got there from the hospital, they all gabbed behind my back, saying: that one there, he won't last. And I heard them, too . . . I got so down. I was thirty years old, I hadn't even turned thirty-one yet, I had my operation three days before I turned thirty-one. That was forty-nine years ago.

When I got a little bit better, I met a couple from here, from Miranda, at the shelter – they'd come up from the south of Angola to spend Christmastime in Luanda. They told me to head on down there, that the land was good and the weather, too, so I packed up all my things and off I went. I left Luanda on the last day of December, 1962, and got to Hoque on the first of January. It was sixty kilometers from Sá da Bandeira – they call it Lubango now. Hoque is a thousand kilometers from Luanda by truck, clunkclunk-clunk . . . I got taken there by a trucker, and he said to me: look here, if you're not doin' so good, I'll be back before too long to pick up some tobacco, you can hitch a ride real easy and meet me in Quilengues and I'll take you to Luanda – that way you can head on back to Portugal. As soon as I picked up a hoe I didn't feel so good, and I thought, I gotta get outta here.

I had five hundred escudos on me, no more than that, but I had asked my sergeant cousin for three contos – speaking in contos. He'd already sent it and I'd set it aside for the trip back. Meanwhile there was this bout of bad weather – even the telephone lines collapsed with all the wind and rain – and all communications got cut. So I stayed.

HER: Eleven months to the day after he got to Angola, that's when I arrived with our three kids, one was six years old, the other four, and the last one still a babe in arms. I went from here to Vimioso, and from Vimioso to Duas Igrejas to take the train to Porto, and in Porto we switched trains and then we went to Lisbon to get on a boat. The only downside to the boat trip was it was so short. It only lasted eleven days,

*and that was the first vacation I ever took in my whole life:
I didn't cook, didn't wash no dishes, all I did was wash the
kids' clothes. I wasn't scared, either. The sea was smooth as
a blanket. I gave the cabin attendant a fat tip, so we weren't
short of food: cheese sandwiches, milk, fruit for the kids, he'd
bring me anything I asked for. The kids said: Mom, Mom,
the boat's gonna sink! And I'd just say to them: no, it won't,
darlings, no, it won't.*

HIM: *Later, a man who died the day I come back here sold
me some land for thirty contos, speaking in contos. I had to
borrow money, even had to pawn my rifle . . . I lived through
eighteen fierce months . . . And then there were even folks
that said: Senhor João, he's a good man, sure, but it'd be
better if he were a bad man – meaning I should've been
different – he's a real good man, but he's got a* chipembe
*there, a bad bit o' land where nothing will grow. We had
us an irrigation ditch and a shack, but no roof. Had Zé
been born yet?*

HER: *No, Zé were born later.*

HIM: *So I built us a roof. We could plant potatoes there and
settle down, our kids and us.*

HER: *We daubed the room and got it all cleaned up real nice.*

HIM [laughing]: *And then it started raining, but as the cob
hadn't set, it rained inside! We were there for a whole other
year. Then I said: I'm gonna build us another shack down
there, where it's proper. And we was there another one, two
years before we finally started harvesting crops and making
a decent living . . .*

HER: *Then we built ourselves a house, and that was that.*

HIM: *We built a real sturdy house. It wasn't nothing fancy, but it was a real nice little place, in a good spot. The porch was kind of like this one, actually.*

HER: *The porch was just like this, yeah.*

HIM: *And then they started saying, Senhor João, now that there's a lucky man. I harvested wheat when folks thought there was no wheat to harvest.*

HER: *We still had to dig plenty more ditches . . .*

HIM: *. . . I ended up irrigating some real good hectares of land. There was one year I harvested one thousand bags of corn weighing around 90 kilos each and fifteen bags of beans weighing 130 kilos each, or maybe even more. We grew potatoes, wheat, corn, and beans. I built myself up a desirable farm there, and bought myself a pick-up, a tractor – I had almost a hundred cattle, and when I was just starting to think of getting a bigger truck . . .*

HER: *. . . They opened up an airlift when decolonization began.*

HIM: *One day one of my kids came up to me and said: look, Pa, our chests aren't made of bronze and if everyone's leaving, we're leaving too . . . There was lines and lines of cars kilometers and kilometers long and they was laden with stuff –* biquátas *as we used to call it – just whatever they had, ready to load onto the boat, or take through South Africa.*

HER: *There were folks even managed to get tractors and trucks through.*

HIM: *A boy from here had a pick-up and a tractor just like mine. He sold his tractor, figured a way of bringing the pick-up back, then managed to start his own business. He did alright for himself, but he's dead now, too.*

HER: *My father used to listen to the radio a lot and he heard what was going on in North Africa and thereabouts . . .*

HIM: *He had sent us a letter saying he didn't want us to write him back, he just wanted us to go get him in Portugal. That there was the only time I come back to Portugal while I was living in Angola. As luck had it, when I got to Bragança it was snowing – I shook in my boots, and my teeth were all clattering . . .*

HER: *. . . And because my father listened to the radio so much, he got this idea in his head that they was killing folks by the dozen and he got scared, so he said: if you don't want to go back to Portugal, I'll go on my own and figure something out for myself. And I told him: now hold your horses, when we go, we'll go together, and if we die, we'll die together, and if they kill us, they'll kill us all together.*

HIM: *One of my men told me: you can't go, boss. I know a place in Quilengues, and you got flour, so take two or three bags of flour there and a sack of fish and then stay there till this here blows over. Alright, I said, and I told him I just had to take my family to Luanda and I'd be right back – I didn't want to have my arm twisted . . . After independence – if things got better – I intended to come back.*

HER: *While we were packing our trunks to take on the boat, three blacks came up to the house . . .*

HIM: *. . . They were part of UNITA, and were fleeing the skirmish in Sá da Bandeira.*

HER: *Folk in Hoque were MPLA and those men, they were from the UNITA and they were on their way to meet the rest, who were in Cacula . . .*

HIM: *About thirty kilometers from there . . .*

HER: *. . . But they weren't taking the roads, they was sticking to the bush. They'd left their uniforms and hidden their guns and then they came knocking at our door. They knocked and I said, what is it? What's going on out there? Senhora, could you spare us some fubá?*

HIM: *They called cornmeal fubá.*

HER: *Sure I can, and I did. I gave them some fish, too. They tried paying me, tried giving me twenty-thousand réis. And I told them no, I don't want nothing, go on, go fill your bellies, go eat in the bush, go, go fill your bellies, 'cause I don't need nothing, not me. I don't know how many times they must've said, may the Lady protect you, may Our Lord keep you, God in heaven protect these good people. My eyes filled with tears.*

HIM: *I couldn't steal from them, take advantage of them. I didn't have it in me. It ain't right of me to say this, but I'll say what I feel: there was folk out there who – I don't even know how to say it . . .*

HER: *. . . Who were thugs.*

HIM: *When it was us who was on their land . . . It was sickening. Them folks went there to set a bad example. And they paid for it with their lives.*

HER: *They killed them.*

HIM: *. . . And they deserved no less, and I'm speaking against our race here. I was the first one there to start paying the men every two weeks. A man who'd been there a long time told me: you must be made o' money to be paying them every two weeks and I said to him: I'll live my life as I please, and*

you can do the same. For the folk who'd lent me money first
I'd even take along my oxen and men to do the sowing, I
had forty to fifty folk working for me at times, but I'd say
to my men that the wheat was for me 'cause the men didn't
want to work for them . . .

HER: *We didn't have any enemies. In the end, they just kept
saying to us: you can't go, boss.*

HIM: *. . . And they'd tell me: even if we wanted to speak up,
we can't – we go talk to the chief, but the white man walks
in and we're left at the door.*

HER: *I never had no trouble while I was on that farm. The
black women always came to me to sell their goods for sugar.
They'd bring me half a dozen eggs, or fruit they'd picked in
the bush for the boys. There was this fourteen-year-old who
worked for us, he looked after the pigs and the chickens and
I'd tell him, Carlos, you go on and talk to them 'cause I don't
know Umbundu. Ask them how much the eggs cost. Nothing,
he'd say, it's just breakfast for you, Senhora.*

HIM: *Then they all killed each other.*

HER: *And it still hasn't been settled, it still ain't really settled.*

HIM: *The young folk in Luanda are rebelling. The south is
calm. Our youngest is there and our oldest son is going
there again soon.*

HER: *They're starting a business, the two brothers. My youngest
son already has his Angolan citizenship. He was there for a
month three years ago, and that's when he got his citizenship.*

HIM: *He threw a party there in the* quimbo, *on our land.
He got 150 folk together and spent like a king. And he even*

made a movie of the party and brought it here to show
us. Everyone dancing, the old folk talking about me. They
had this nickname for me, Berimbindo – 'cause it's like
bem-vindo, welcome, so they called me Berimbindo. Did
Berimbindo uafa? Meaning, did he die? No, my sons said.
Berimbindo is here in my heart, they'd say. I cried watching that movie.

HIM: *She even had the smarts to bake a batch of bread before
we left. We managed to fill our bellies even then.*
HER: *I baked a whole bag of bread.*
HIM: *And that was real bread. First-rate flour, made by hand . . .*
HER: *We left the key to our house with our buddy – we were
his daughter's godparents.*
HIM: *He was mulatto anyway.*
HER: *We left him the cattle, the goats, the tractor – everything!*
HIM: *And seeds!*
HER: *Yeah, seeds. We said to him: the land here's sown, so go
and harvest some for yourself and then when I come back,
all you gotta do is give me the seeds so I can sow too. Every-
thing was just right, we had worked everything out real nice,
but then he didn't write us and we never did write him . . .*
HIM: *The mail was cut off then.*
HER: *. . . They didn't let mail get in or out and we never heard
from him again.*
HIM: *Then a black came through and killed him, out of
envy. And our goddaughter, she was eleven years old,
lightning struck our house and killed her. It wrecked most
of our home.*

HER: *And then the whole house fell down. Our kids, they took a picture of it for us and then showed it to me – the only thing that survived was the stove chimney.*

HIM: *It was October when we got here. Our eldest son stayed behind to load the last of the containers onto the boat. It was real little, almost nothing, really, but still my most valuable one got stolen. I even went down to Lisbon, to the Cais da Rocha . . . but I couldn't find it. Folk welcomed us here, in the village. They brought us nine bags of potatoes – and that was just the potatoes. I knew what folk said about us* retornados *coming back from Africa, most of them.*

HER: *And some still say it today.*

HIM: *I miss looking out at my land. Sometimes I'd go outside just to look at everything I'd planted.*

HER: *We had a big farm. We'd look at treetops out there in the distance, and it was all ours. If I was twenty years younger, I'd be back there, sure I would. The weather was real good where we lived: none too hot, none too cold. And the land is blessed – everything we planted grew. Here, all the work I've got . . . Just today I went and checked on the beans and they're no good, they're falling off their stalks. The weather here spoils everything.*

HIM: *I don't want to go see it now. I cared for that land – and the thought of going there and seeing how it is now . . . But that's life . . . When good fortune finally smiles down on you . . . Here, I at least had a few things to my name, so I said, alright, this is where we'll stay. Now, my sons, they say to me, we shouldn't've come up here, the ones who stayed in Lisbon, they're doing better for themselves, but my things were here, my olive trees, my vegetable gardens – I had a place to live here, where else could I have gone?*

HIM: *I stopped working a year and a half ago, when this trouble with my bladder started. I used to make my own wine, grow my own potatoes and olive trees. I still got some olive trees, but I don't look after them no more. It ain't worth it. Growing things today, no matter what you try to grow, it just don't pay. I don't know where this country's heading. They're encouraging folk not to work, not to produce . . .*

HER: *Now everyone's got their 230 or 240 euros . . .*

HIM: *But there's lots of poor folk, right?*

HER: *. . . I never thought they'd give me the little they do. So long as we keep getting the small pension they give us . . .*

HIM: *We've made our nest. It's the bird that's dead. Its wings won't fly.*

HER: *He's always complaining. He's been complaining for twenty years now! I'm sicker than he is, but you don't see me kicking up a fuss.*

HIM: *No one believes in old sufferings.*

HER [laughing]: *You're an old man now, you can't get no older than old. It's a sad life for a couple of folk like us. Our kids come over for the August festival, but then they go back to their own lives. The two of us, we're stuck here, but at least we can still talk to each other. If there was just one of us left, we'd have nothing to do but stare at the walls.*

HIM: *I'm scared she'll die first. That's what really haunts me.*

HER: *I'm eighty-five already, going on eighty-six. My legs grow heavier each day. They don't want to walk. I got pain and pain and more pain. But we just gotta keep on.*

HIM: *If she goes first, I don't know what I'll . . .*

HER: *Oh, you'll go to an old folks' home. What else can you do? And if there ain't a bed for you there, you can just come on here and sleep at home.*

HIM: *A man gets used to sleeping in a good bed, to having decent clothes and a decent towel, to sleeping next to his wife . . .*

HER: *What he don't want is to die.*

HIM: *. . . What's an old man to do, sick and alone?*

HIM: *Lazarus had been dead for four days. And Jesus said: let's see what we can do. And He said: I am life and I am death, do you believe? And He said: move that rock. And then He said: Lazarus, rise! And Lazarus rose. And so did Jesus, and they say we all rise again. Lazarus and Jesus came back after just two or three days, but we only will after millions of years . . . What I learned in the cradle I'll only forget in my grave. My parents gave me this faith, it's the only one I know. Me, I think there's something after death. It's just this feeling I got. They put so much fear in us – why'd they have been fooling us? I don't know, though. The dead don't write, they don't call – there's just no way of knowing.*

HIM [watching night fall]: *The moon's just the same in Angola.*

HER: *And the stars. Sometimes I was there and it was like I was still here, just looking up.*

ELISA AND SARA

Sometimes I imagine Elisa painting. She has long black hair and narrow shoulders; her back is to me and it's as if she herself were part of the picture, and as though the portrait she is painting, the painting within the painting, were unfinished, still in the process of creating itself.

The truth is Elisa hasn't painted in years, though a part of her still creates images – she can't live otherwise – and maybe that's why I picture her painting, hoping that perhaps, after her father's death, she has taken it up again. Those who don't have faith find comfort in ideas beyond heaven, and Elisa believes fervently in humanity's capacity to create.

Or maybe I always picture her within a painting because, be it in Trás-os-Montes, where her parents chose to move when she was still young, or in Porto, where she was born and where she later returned, she never seemed to belong anywhere I saw her. After living a while in the small town of Mogadouro, her parents decided to move somewhere even smaller. And so they bought a house in a village: a house her father had

single-handedly renovated from top to bottom. It was in
that house that I often spoke to Elisa. Later – her father
had died by then – I met up with her in Porto, in the
apartment she had just moved into with her boyfriend.
The apartment was in a narrow building with steep stairs
leading up to a top floor that felt claustrophobic rather
than spacious. The building was located in the center of
Porto, on a square with a forgotten air about it, like so
many other squares and streets in the center of Portugal's
second most important city. I visited her on a public holi-
day and there were very few people out on the streets.
A couple of kids played ball listlessly. Elisa was fixing up
her apartment, trying to make it match her sensibility
as closely as possible. Yet she already seemed to know
that, despite all her effort, it still wouldn't be the right
setting for her. I pictured her leaving again and starting
up somewhere new, in a big city perhaps, since she pos-
sessed the intensity of large metropolises. She reminded
me of a character who had not yet found her story.

The first time I saw her she was at her father's bedside.
I was moved by the way she touched him, by the way
she squeezed his hand. Every time she spoke, she would
wait for an answer. She didn't expect him to moan or
sigh or to make any other strange new sound – the
sounds of sickness – but instead expected to hear him
as she hoped to later remember him.

Their youngest cat, Nicha, leapt onto the bed and
tried to nestle in between her father's legs. Elisa shooed

her away affectionately. Her mother wandered around the room with a fly swatter and, whenever a fly landed on Elisa's father, she killed it, not knowing if he could feel a thing.

In the room, there was an articulated bed for the patient and, beside it, the bed where his wife slept. Those were wearying nights, and recently his wife had been going to sleep convinced that was the night her husband would die. Then, after waking up and checking to see if he was breathing, she'd think of how he might not make it to the end of the day.

Lately, in the night and during the day, he'd been waking up from dreams or from hallucinations – it was hard to tell them apart – and speaking of Porto, his hometown. He'd ask when they were going to leave.

In the room, a television stood on a table, always on and always muted; next to it were family photos, and amongst them a photo of the couple standing against a Trás-os-Montes landscape. They are still young in the photograph, which could have been taken on one of their first trips to the region, when they fell in love with the land and made the decision to move there.

I never saw Elisa against a Trás-os-Montes landscape and I can't picture her in the countryside. The truth is we never met outside and, because of her doll-white skin, I can't help but picture her indoors. In the photos of her scattered around the house, the backdrops are impossible to make out. That close-up of her that hangs in the kitchen, from when she was very young, back when she was a goth – short spiked hair, collar around her neck, heavy eye make-up – could have been taken in a studio.

That day and then a few days later, we talked at the kitchen table. Her mother was always nearby, sitting down and getting up again, wandering between the kitchen and the bedroom. Behind Elisa there was a door that led to the garage, which was her father's workshop and where he had spent his stronger hours. Her father had not yet died, but it already felt haunted.

To Elisa's left was the front door, which friends and neighbors would often knock on to ask after Senhor Rui. There was also a first-floor entrance, which led to stairs that flanked the outside of the house.

Elisa's father was a contractor and known for being good at his job. He'd only hand clients the keys to their houses once he was certain there was nothing left to be done. The owner would walk in and find their home finished, perfect. Yet his own house never would be; he'd left things half-done, imperfect. That little window, to Elisa's right, on the wall above the kitchen counter, was one of his last jobs. The hatch let light from the kitchen into the other ground-floor room. He didn't know then that they would one day have to turn that room into a bedroom because he would no longer be able to walk up the stairs to his own bedroom on the upper floor.

Scene: mother and daughter at the kitchen table. Now and then, in the silence, when they stop speaking, they can hear him. (Or is it the sound of his illness?) The other daughter is missing.

Sara was on her way. She drove alone. And she cried the whole way from France to Portugal, the road distant, distorted, a desert.

Along the staircase hang pictures Elisa painted when she was younger and had not yet decided she would not be an artist, but a lawyer. One is a self-portrait of a woman with long black hair and large eyes. The background is once again abstract and, if I remember correctly, blue, a shade that might mean night or day.

We walked up to the first floor. It was Saturday night and Elisa had decided to throw a dinner party, to fill the house with people and noise: a regular occurrence on weekends. No one was allowed to be sad on her watch, not while her father was still alive. She also thought that perhaps her father could, if not hear, at least feel the party, and that he would like the idea that life was still going on around him. But it was the guests who could hear him from the floor below. The family called those sounds wind. 'He's howling,' they'd say.

He was the main topic of conversation throughout most of the dinner. The guests painted a portrait of a charismatic man who hadn't had an education, but who had learned all the same. A man who loved people, who would leave the house and not return until hours later, having stopped to speak to everyone he met. He had lived as few others had, with real resolve, and he would die in the same way. He didn't want his doctors to fool him or lie to him, to omit or downplay the gravity of his illness. He knew exactly what was happening to him. He was dying.

At dinner, they ate seafood rice, consumed multiple bottles of vinho verde and made enough of a racket to scandalize the neighbors. At times, her mother would ask for some quiet and, even though she couldn't tell whether her husband was calling her, she'd walk downstairs to comfort him, to reposition his legs, or simply to see him. No one knew whether, in those moments when he was more lucid, he could sense the more-or-less forced cheerfulness on the floor above him. But Elisa knew those moments of lucidity were the worst for him. One of the images she would never live to forget was this: the brief but eloquent look in her father's eyes whenever he became aware of the situation he was in.

Without meaning to, they would speak of him in the past tense. I never knew him, what a pity, they'd say. The man they described was not the man in that bed.

There was something literary about that description. As a matter of fact, the family itself seemed to have been lifted from a novel. Both daughters had left home after arguments with their parents, both had fought for their father's recognition, both had returned. The older sister, Sara, only made up with her father after he fell ill, and that lost time had aged her. It was not so much that their family history seemed improbable, and therefore more convincing when turned into fiction; it was the way in which matters of life or death had altered the family's composition.

Sara had once been a hairdresser but now worked with her husband in France. They installed transmission towers along the highway. In the same way she once took note of people's hair, a quirk of the trade, now, as she drove, she couldn't help but notice the towers along the highway and the electrical wires that cut across the windows and against the sky or the land.

After dinner, feeling slightly tipsy, Elisa showed me the room she'd lived in as a teenager. On the walls hung photos of her posing with friends, cutouts of exhibitions she had participated in, and even an article from a national newspaper about how odd it was for a young goth to be staging an exhibition in Mogadouro, one of Portugal's most remote towns. The room felt nostalgic to her now because, at thirty-one, she felt she could no longer exhibit herself so brazenly on the walls; or perhaps it seemed particularly nostalgic to me because, being little older than Elisa, I had long felt embarrassed about putting my own world on display.

As we walked down the stairs, I noticed the painting again, the long black hair. Elisa and her dark mane walked down the steps in front of me, without saying a word. I didn't know if the picture had been painted many years ago or just a few, but it seemed to me a portrait of Elisa now and not one of her at the time it had been painted.

Would Sara drive through the night, or stop to sleep along the way? Either way, she would feel afraid in the night.

The picture I imagine Elisa painting with her back to me, this unfinished portrait, could be as much a portrait of herself as one of her father. I'm reminded of those nineteenth-century photographers who would photograph bodies at the moment life left them, their eyes still open. These portraits would then be placed alongside earlier photographs, creating a certain continuity between the living and the dead. With the magical new technology of daguerreotypes, photographers could even make the dead visible long after the body itself had disappeared. They made white, chalky figures appear in family portraits, at times no more than a veil hovering over the image, a form of communication both artificial and sincere.

Sara was afraid of waking up to find her father had died during the night and that she had not made it in time to say goodbye. In any case, she knew that even if she did make it – and even if he lasted months instead of weeks, and she kept returning, on time, every fortnight – there would still always be something left to say.

*

It was daybreak when Elisa hugged me at the door. She asked after my father and told me to enjoy his company as much as I could. Nursing a hangover the following day, what struck me the most from the night before was the conversation we'd had by her front door, just as I was leaving. I couldn't stop thinking of how – and it had always been clear – we are the others.

That week, Sara made it in time to see her father alive, but not to speak with him as they had spoken before. He was incomprehensible. No one could tell whether the drugs were making him hallucinate, whether he was asleep and dreaming, or whether this was just the way men died.

I never met him – 'What a pity,' Sara said. She, the older daughter, once again described an exceptional man, but one who would only be remembered by his family and, for a while at least, in the village and in Mogadouro. All I could see was a body lying on a bed.

When Sara arrived, Elisa had already left for Ovar, where she interned at a courthouse. The two sisters didn't cross paths, but in some strange way it was as if they were always together, and I can't think of one without remembering the other. They were almost opposites, almost rivals, but they shared the intensity of difficult love.

Sara was not as I had pictured her: a face of sharp corners, almost cubist, more fraught than her sister's, and even her mother's.

And so now it's Sara and her mother who are in the kitchen, and Elisa who is missing from the scene.

The last time I visited the village of Figueira, just a few weeks before Rui Ferreira's death at the age of fifty-six, Sara showed me her father's office. On his desk stood a computer, and on the shelves stood books, family photos, and Topo Gigio dolls. He'd been nicknamed Topo Gigio and he liked the name so much he'd had business cards printed with the tv puppet on them. Instead of the name 'Ferreira' there was a picture of a big-eared mouse on the mailbox next to his front door.

After their father's death and after the funeral, Sara stopped traveling between France and Portugal every fortnight. And yet I still can't help but picture her in a car, permanently in transit. She never stops leaving.

Later, the house in Figueira was left vacant, a still life.

Last time I saw Elisa, she was wearing a tank top and jeans. Her hands were dirty and the toolbox lay open – she'd just finished installing a shower in the bathroom of their new apartment in Porto. The afternoon light struck the dust floating in the living room, making it visible, magical. It was very hot on that early October day and her mother sat on the sofa fanning herself with a magazine. She was tired. She had slept poorly, having dreamt her husband wanted to go back to work again and that he was angry with her for having thrown away his work clothes.

As we spoke, Elisa lit one cigarette after another. Nicha, the cat, crawled into her lap, and Elisa petted her as she talked about her father and about the details of his funeral without once saying: death, died, dead. I kept hearing the words she'd said that morning, standing at her front door in Figueira: we are the others.

SARA

I've cried a lot over being so far away. I spent all those years claiming I didn't miss a thing. I'd come to Portugal once a year, because I had to. I'd come to see my parents, not the country.

In my head, my parents were young. I couldn't picture them being old. If my dad was eighty, like my father-in-law, who died recently, I'd think, well, that's normal . . . If he was old. But he isn't old. My dad's always been in good shape. I even thought that maybe he was just making it all up to see if I really loved him. That he'd asked my mother to lie to me – to see if I'd come, because we'd been fighting.

I don't believe you,

that's what I'd say to him, to keep him quiet, to stop him from telling me those things. And he'd say

look, it might be this or it might be that

and I'd say

no, no, no, it's nothing.

Then he read me his test results. I came back here, to visit him, convinced it wasn't true. And I could see he wasn't well, but he didn't seem as sick as they'd said. As far as I was concerned, it was everything but cancer – that was impossible. I don't know how it was that I woke up one day and saw things for how they really were. My dad's always grabbed the bull by the horns. It was us who didn't want to face the facts. He wanted us to cooperate, but we just wanted to hold on to hope. Not that he'd be saved, necessarily, but that he'd at least live a few more years. We'd heard of people with his kind of cancer who'd carried on living for two or three years – or even four or five more. We're always waiting on a miracle. Like, what if tomorrow there's a test that shows he's been cured? Even though the doctors are always saying there is no cure . . . But we just carry on hoping for a miracle.

He made us plan his funeral. In the beginning it seemed ridiculous, but it was out of the question to go against him. He got us all together here and he asked

   what kind of funeral do you want me to have?

   a regular funeral?

   a cremation?

It was unheard of, what he was doing. He wanted to know what we thought, but he never expressed his own opinions. I said

   if it were up to me, I wouldn't cremate you.

   My sister said

   I can't get my head around the idea of cremation, but it's cleaner and I can't help picturing bugs in the ground.

   He wanted to see if he could get us to agree.

   Do you want it to be here?

   in Figueira?

   or in Mogadouro?

   It didn't make sense for it to be in Porto – we'd left so many years ago . . .

   Did we want there to be a mass?

   a priest?

   We talked about it in the same way we talked about everything. Me and my sister went to speak to the man at the funeral parlor. He was a friend of my dad's, but he said he didn't like to go to people's homes, he said when they see me, they immediately think business, and I don't have the heart to go see Rui.

But my dad wasn't the kind to send messages. He wanted to speak to him in person, so the man from the funeral parlor ended up coming over. They spent a few minutes in his room – I was on the phone to France, my mother was busy with guests – and suddenly everything was settled. He'd planned everything. I felt like crawling into a hole. Sitting with my dad and hearing him talking to this man about his own funeral . . .

He was in control of everything until the end. Now he can't control anything anymore. Yesterday, when I got home, he didn't recognize me. It was so painful. Every time I came home from France, he would get really excited. My sister would say

I'm actually kind of jealous, Dad never cries when I come home.

The last time, he clung onto me and cried, and he said

stay here, I'm never letting you go.

I felt like my trips home brought him strength, like he was holding on to see me. This time I'd hoped to bring him just a little more courage again. On the phone, I'd always say to him

just one week to go now

just two days to go now

I'll be on my way tomorrow

I thought he'd be waiting for me, that he'd be full of energy. I was looking forward to seeing his reaction . . . If only for just a few more days, or even just one more day . . . He's seen that I'm here, but, the state he's in, I don't know if he can remember: he forgets everything from one minute to the next.

*

My mom lives with this night and day. I come and I'm here for a week. She's been living with this for months. At his worst, he can spend days on end like this, half-unconscious. My mom, she's got to listen to him moan in pain all night long. She chose to keep sharing a room with him. It's not a choice just any woman would make. I respect her even more for that – I didn't know she was capable of making such a sacrifice.

They always told me I was like my mom and my sister was like my dad, and I always wanted to be like my dad. And my dad said that him and my sister were made of the same stuff, and that created a kind of rivalry between us – and jealousy . . . The more they told me I was like my mom, the more I'd get annoyed and want to be like him. I always wanted to show everyone I could be as strong and smart as he was. That I could be stubborn like him and never leave anything half-done. I wanted to be a daughter who deserved a father like him – and to be like him.

You could write a book about my dad. No matter what he said, it was always interesting. He'd talk to judges, to maids. He didn't have any enemies; he never got upset. People always asked him for advice: they needed to know what he thought. He was never boring, never over the top. I knew people liked my dad, but I never knew how much. Having twenty people around on any given day is nothing. People are always bumping into each other here. They've got to wait their turn. There were times when there'd be people around till eleven at night. They're living through this with us. The other day, when I was

*visiting Mogadouro, I bumped into someone who'd lost more
than one relative to cancer and I felt so awful. I thought: 'You
lost your dad too and I never said anything.'*

*I didn't give a damn. I just didn't care. I never liked going
to funerals, so I just never bothered. We're all selfish. Only now
do I value sharing this suffering with people, being comforted
by them – people are always comforting me these days – everywhere I go.*

*Whenever I had to ask for advice, to help me make a deci-
sion, my first instinct was always to ask my dad. His opinion
was the one that mattered. Mom always agreed with him. My
mom's the one who took care of us at home: buying shoes when
we needed them, doing our homework, teaching us to cook or
to darn socks; she had to deal with the hard stuff. He taught us
about morals. He had this amazing life philosophy – and without
having ever gone to school. He was such a chatterbox. He spent
hours and hours of his life talking to me and my sister. And it
was normal – the things he said, they'd sink in, and now that
we've grown up, we do things we didn't even know we had in
us, but that, little by little, have stuck. He taught us to be sure
of where we stood – to dance, but to always know where we
put our feet. It was only when I realized I was losing him that
I started appreciating what he taught us. I was always really
proud of my dad, but I never told him. We never had much
time just to ourselves. Whenever I'd come over from France,
the whole family would be around. Guests coming in and out
of the house. The phone ringing off the hook. But I'd find a way
for us to be alone, and still I couldn't tell him. I wanted to, but
it just wouldn't come out. I so needed to tell him how sorry I*

was – for the war I'd waged against him to prove I was just as strong, if not stronger, than he was. I know he understood. Last time, before I left, I had to tell him

I'm proud of you.

If anything, I didn't tell him enough. I didn't have the time, living so far away. What I didn't do then I can't do now. He can't hear me anymore.

I'm driving and it already hurts to think of how I'll arrive and then have to leave again. It's not like living in Porto or in Lisbon, which are sort of near. If I could just press pause on everything over there . . . Just for a month or two, and take it easy. I could be here to support my mom, to take over for her. I feel like I'm just not enough, that maybe I should be doing more for them. I even blame myself for having moved to France. I'd counted on leaving and never coming back. Now I think

why'd I decide to go so far?

And what about when my mom's turn comes, when she's old . . .

why'd I go so far away?

But life goes on. I come back as often as I can, but going back and forth so much is exhausting, and then there are the expenses and the risks involved in driving so many kilometers. My husband says

you'll make me a widower, too.

There's no way of knowing how long you'll be in this kind of situation. We don't know if it'll be today or if it'll be tomorrow or really soon. If we knew when, it'd be easier to manage, if we could just predict it . . . I'm afraid something bad will happen to him while I'm away. When I'm in France, I can't stop wondering

is he breathing?

I'll spend hours like that. When the phone rings, I shudder. When it doesn't ring, I just stare at it

it's going to ring.

I'm fixated on things – it's crazy. I think

I'm just here, relaxing, smoking my cigarette and drinking coffee, and right now my mom might be screaming by his side.

I'm scared of enjoying life while all this is happening. My mom knows to call me immediately. And I can't stop planning the trip back. I'm obsessed with that moment. I'm both scared for it to happen and just waiting for it to happen. I tell my son

get everything ready, we might have to leave at any moment, pack your bags, grab some clothes, 'cause when I call you, no matter what time it is, even at night, I'm going to come pick you up.

I'm also drilling that sense of urgency into him to see if maybe he'll realize he's going to lose his grandfather. When I lost my grandparents, I didn't even blink. I tell him to call his granddad, I tell him

watch out, 'cause the day you feel like calling him, he won't be around anymore.

Like everyone, I think I love my father more than other people love theirs.

I love my dad so much I'd do anything for him. I'd give my life for him. But there's nothing I can do. It's horrible because

I like fixing everything. I was never the kind to throw in the towel. I've always managed to find an answer to everything. But what's that worth? He's always had an answer for everything, but not for this. Neither do I. We think we control everything, but we don't control anything at all.

ELISA

The nurses realized it was almost time, so they called my sister and me. We made it. We even got to spend a day and a half with him, except he was already unconscious – I mean, sedated. Everyone was ready for it to happen, everyone but me. I just sat there, acting like nothing was happening, cracking jokes. And when it happened, my mom and my sister started screaming. And I couldn't react. It must have been two months before I cried. It's really hard for me to cry. And now I've finally started crying, but only because I'll get all worked up over something minor, and then I might cry a little out of frustration. But when it happened – and the atmosphere at our house was just so strange . . . It took me a long time to realize what was going on.

And those memories are so awful. The worst ones are from the last days. I'd almost rather not have seen anything. They've got nothing to do with him. It's not the same person. I can't erase them and I can't deal with them either. I see my dad, sick and suffering – he's stretching his fingers, wracked with pain, screaming. It was hard for me to believe it was that bad. It was always hard for me to believe he was in pain. These days, when I'm in pain, when my knee hurts, for example, I'll feel that pain and then I'll start imagining it being much more intense, and all over my body. I beat myself up a lot. I try to imagine how it feels . . . When I lie down, when I'm in bed, I wake up in the middle of the night and my body is half-asleep, still half sleeping, and right then, when my body's like that, I start picturing what it must be like to feel that way for a full

twenty-four hours, then another twenty-four hours and another
twenty-four hours . . . I try to feel what he felt.

And what was going through his head?
It haunts me so, so much:
what does someone who's dying think about?
does he believe he's going to die?
does he believe it all the time?
is it a constant thought?
isn't it?
does he try to kid himself?
what happens?
how does he see other people?
does he try picturing what everyone else's life will be like?
does he think about what he's going to lose?

I can't really picture death, much less when it comes to my
dad. But now I have that image of him lying there stretched
out, white and cold and so different to what he was really like.
And then they go pick up a coffin and they put your person in
the coffin. And that's so strange to me. All I wanted was to hit
the man who took the coffin away. We're so medieval about it.
Death itself seems medieval. You put a person in a box. And he's
in there, all bunched up. Just there. And then the old women
come see him and kiss him and pray and cry. I reacted very
badly to having other people see my dad. I didn't want anyone
to be there. I saw all that mess . . . It happened at home, in that
little room where his bed was, that was where . . . And the man,
he brought in a coffin, but the first coffin was too small and
so he was standing around there, with my dad . . . Then they
went to get another coffin and they were just walking around

like that! They went to pry him out of the first coffin and put
him in another one. All I could do was watch them and think
to myself, that's a coffin and it's small, and then they went and
got another one. And then they set everything up, and they held
what people call a wake. And my dad spent the whole night
there. In my head, we all went to bed and my dad was sleeping,
too, and everything was alright. I just couldn't acknowledge it,
even after everything I'd seen. But the worst part, the absolute
worst, was when they came to pick him up. They came in and
it felt as if they'd just stopped by to pick something up from a
store. These are the images I live with. It's the same day after
day, they come by and say 'it's time,' and they take him.

'It's time?'

When they came to take him away, my world collapsed. I
saw the hearse outside and all those people on the street and
it was just horrible . . . I had this urge to hold him, to hold
my dad . . . And that's when I realized what had happened.
He made this sound . . . And the air inside him went into my
mouth and I almost threw up. That's when it clicked. Because
I don't really just accept things, I never have, like, my whole
life. And at that moment, I got it.

They put up tripods in the cemetery to rest the coffin on. Since
we're not religious, we didn't have a priest. Our friends spoke.
It was really beautiful, more beautiful than anything any priest
could've said – they never make any sense. First my dad's
friend spoke, then I did. I don't know how, but I spoke loud, so
everyone could hear me. From what I've been told, I was calm
and I spoke well. I explained why there hadn't been a mass

and said something along the lines of: my dad's religion was love and friendship and that's all anyone needs to be happy.

My dad was put in a niche. I wasn't about to let them put him in the ground. My dad – down in the ground like an animal? No. Niches, they're nice and clean. They're made of concrete and my dad really liked concrete. And they put the person at eye level. It's clean. It's still not a twenty-first century thing, but it's halfway there. 'Cause something's got to change. One day we'll have to figure out a new solution.

In the next few days, I didn't notice a thing, I did everything mechanically – I just went and dealt with everything

> *what needs doing?*
> *what needs doing?*

We needed to handle the paperwork and go to the funeral parlor and order letters to spell out his name on the niche and all those awful things you have to do. Clean the house. See who needs paying, check whether we owed the pharmacy any money, or anyone else. And then I went back to Ovar and my mom went with me. I went back to work. It was hard to go back to court, to face people. They'd come up to me and ask how I was and I'd tell them not to ask. He'd pop into my head from time to time, but I'd fight it. But after a while – that's when it got really bad. I don't know how long it took . . . The other day, I had to stop and ask myself when it had happened, because I couldn't remember what day it had been. I know people normally memorize these dates, but I couldn't remember the day – I couldn't even remember the month

was it June or July?
was it August?

I'm reacting very strangely, the littlest things make me want to scream. It's not that I want to start sobbing or anything. I feel like hitting people. One day, this little old man came to the courthouse to complain, he was fifty-something, sixty. I went to talk to him, I was being friendly, and he just started whining, 'cause he's broke and he's got so many problems and his son is getting his master's degree, and he's worried he won't be able to pay for his son's master's, and it just started getting to me. And I said to him: 'Look, you need to go to a lawyer and do this and do that.' And he wouldn't listen to me and he just kept on whining. And that started messing with me, I looked at that bastard and thought to myself

you son of a bitch. Do you even know what real problems are?

I pictured punching him. All I know is that I looked at that man and felt such hatred . . . I just had to say to him: 'You have no idea what real problems are, get out of here! You're lucky you're alive and that you have a son who's getting his master's!' And I kicked him out of there. And everyone was staring at me. As soon as I sat down, these tears, nervous tears, started running down my face, they weren't out of sadness, they were just tears of anger, and they wouldn't stop falling. With my mother and my boyfriend, it's always on the cards. Everything they do annoys me. Everything they don't do annoys me. Everything they say, the way they say it, annoys me. It's like I'm constantly boiling up inside, while also trying to be reasonable and thinking:

but how is any of this their fault?

I try to be rational, but there's a part of me that needs them to understand. And then, when I stop thinking about myself and I think about my mother, I wonder

how is she doing?

She must be so much worse off than me, and then I think I'm never going to give her a hard time again, never again, and then I see her and she says something and I explode.

I try to keep calm and get everything done. It takes a lot of effort, so much effort. I still haven't passed my law exams, my future seems so uncertain, and even though I believe strongly in so many things, my future seems really far away, like I've pressed pause on it. I don't have a job yet, and I don't have my dad to give me a hand. My mom was never independent, never had a job. It's not going to be easy for her to get her life back together. She needs me. I feel like there's this huge weight on me. I'm trying to do everything and organize everything. And I feel as though I'm failing, and I do stupid stuff sometimes, which really annoys me.

I miss my dad the most when I can't fix a situation. Even if he couldn't fix it himself . . . But whenever I'm upset, I immediately think of my dad. My dad was the one I'd talk to, the one who'd say the right things. And that – that's when I miss him. And so I think that the only thing I can do is try and make things run smoothly. And try to get everything done.

When I started the whole deal of moving to Porto, I had to face the facts because my dad would've been the one to help me out.

*He would've been the one to fix everything up in the apartment.
I brought tools with me. The first holes I tried making, they . . .
I was so anxious . . . I'm getting things done . . . In the beginning, I'd be doing something by myself and I'd feel like my dad
was by my side, as if I was doing these things with him, and
that gave me strength: because I pretended I still had my dad.
I pretended night and day, all the time. But then it all started
feeling distant. And I couldn't pretend all that well anymore.
And now something strange has started happening – it's like
he's inside me. I know it's nothing paranormal, that it's all in
my head, but even so it's really strange. I'll be kneeling, laying
down some mortar, or hammering something, or tightening a
screw . . . Or I'll have put the wall anchor in and I'll be tightening it . . . And the way I hold the screwdriver, the way I breathe,
the expressions I make from the effort, everything, everything
I do feels like how my dad would do it. It's like he's inside me.*

*I'm really selfish when it comes to my dad. My dad is mine. I
was the one who knew him. And sometimes, when it comes to
my mom, I'll say: 'Ok, you're the one who was married to him
for thirty years, but there's a lot about my dad that only I knew.'
I was the one who knew what he liked. Of course it's kind of sub-
conscious, but it's like I want our relationship to be untouchable.*

*My dad died in peace because he lived a full life. And that brings
me peace. Now I always think about how anything can happen,
at any moment, so you've got to make the most of it.*

If I ever have a son, I'll name him Rui.

WHEN YOU COME BACK
FROM THE JOURNEY NO HEALTHY
PERSON WANTS TO TAKE, YOU WILL . . .

watch the clock and finally see time passing;

know you are a machine and not feel saddened but, rather, liberated by the thought;

read obituaries about anonymous deaths and feel responsible, as if you'd known them;

remember those you've lost who did not die a good death and promise yourself it will never happen again;

make sense of the frantic makeup of your days;

share the corniest things you can remember with those closest to you;

want to get married and have children if you have not yet done so, and if you have, spend more time with them;

feel strong, since it will become clear that to do so all you need is to be alive;

want to amend the future if you can no longer amend the past;

live uninterruptedly, like nature;

rather than believe the world ends with each death, believe that, with each birth, the world begins anew.

ACKNOWLEDGMENTS

I would like to thank the Calouste Gulbenkian Foundation for supporting the writing of this book and its first Portuguese edition. I would especially like to thank Jorge Soares, Director of the Gulbenkian Programme for Innovation in Health, for believing in my work and in the value of sharing these issues and stories with a larger audience.

I am indebted to the Home Palliative Care team working in the Planalto Mirandês, Trás-os-Montes, for so generously allowing me to be a part of their routine, and particularly to Doctor Jacinta Fernandes, who welcomed me like an old friend.

The patients and families who feature in this book spoke to me with extraordinary openness, unexpected trust and admirable courage: thank you all so much.

Special thanks to photographer André Cepeda for being my travel companion in Trás-os-Montes and for his unforgettable images.

I could not have completed this book without my friend and fellow writer Alexandra Lucas Coelho, my friend Bárbara Gomes, who is a leading researcher in palliative care, and my family: thank you.

Dear readers,

We rely on subscriptions from people like you to tell these other stories – the types of stories most publishers consider too risky to take on.

Our subscribers don't just make the books physically happen. They also help us approach booksellers, because we can demonstrate that our books already have readers and fans. And they give us the security to publish in line with our values, which are collaborative, imaginative and "shamelessly literary."

All of our subscribers:

- receive a first-edition copy of each of the books they subscribe to
- are thanked by name at the end of these books
- are warmly invited to contribute to our plans and choice of future books

BECOME A SUBSCRIBER, OR GIVE A SUBSCRIPTION TO A FRIEND

Visit andotherstories.org/subscribe to become part of an alternative approach to publishing.

Subscriptions are:

£20 for two books per year

£35 for four books per year

£50 for six books per year

OTHER WAYS TO GET INVOLVED

If you'd like to know about upcoming events and reading groups (our foreign-language reading groups help us choose books to publish, for example) you can:

- join the mailing list at: andotherstories.org/join-us
- follow us on Twitter: @andothertweets
- join us on Facebook: facebook.com/AndOtherStoriesBooks
- follow our blog: Ampersand

This book was made possible thanks to the support of:

Aaron McEnery
Abigail Miller
Adam Butler
Adam Lenson
AG Hughes
Aileen-Elizabeth
    Taylor
Ajay Sharma
Alan Ramsey
Alasdair Thomson
Alastair Gillespie
Alastair Laing
Alastair Maude
Alec Begley
Alex Gregory
Alex Martin
Alex Ramsey
Alex Sutcliffe
Alexander Balk
Alexandra Buchler
Alexandra Georgescu
Alexandra de
    Verseg-Roesch
Alice Nightingale
Alice Toulmin
Alison Bowyer
Alison Hughes
Alison Layland
Alison Smith
Allison Graham
Allyson Dowling
Alyse Ceirante
Amanda Dalton
Amanda DeMarco
Amanda Jane Stratton
Amelia Dowe
Amy Allebone-Salt
Amy Rushton

Anderson Tepper
Andrew Cowan
Andrew Lees
Andrew Marston
Andrew McDougall
Andrew van der Vlies
Andrew Whitelegg
Andy Madeley
Angus MacDonald
Angus Walker
Ann Van Dyck
Anna Dear
Anna Holmwood
Anna Milsom
Anna Solovyev
Anna Vinegrad
Anna-Karin Palm
Anne Carus
Anne Lawler
Anne Marie Jackson
Anne Meadows
Annie McDermott
Antonia Lloyd-Jones
Antonio de Swift
Antony Pearce
Aoife Boyd
Archie Davies
Asako Serizawa
Audrey Holmes

Barbara Anderson
Barbara Mellor
Barbara Robinson
Barry Hall
Bartolomiej Tyszka
Belinda Farrell
Ben Schofield
Ben Smith

Ben Thornton
Benjamin Judge
Benjamin Morris
Bianca Jackson
Bill Myers
Blanco
Blanka Stoltz
Bob Hill
Bob
    Richmond-Watson
Brendan McIntyre
Briallen Hopper
Brian Rogers
Brigita Ptackova

C Mieville
Candy Says Juju
    Sophie
Carl Emery
Carla Coppola
Caroline Rucker
Carolyn A Schroeder
Catherine Mansfield
Catherine Taylor
Catrin Ashton
Cecilia Rossi &
    Iain Robinson
Charles Lambert
Charles Rowley
Charlotte Holtam
Charlotte Murrie &
    Stephen Charles
Charlotte Whittle
Chris Day
Chris Elcock
Chris Fawson
Chris Holmes
Chris Lintott

Chris Stevenson
Chris Vardy
Chris Watson
Chris Wood
Christine Carlisle
Christine Luker
Christopher Allen
Christopher Terry
Ciara Ní Riain
Claire Brooksby
Claire Fuller
Claire Seymour
Claire Tranah
Claire Williams
Clarissa Botsford
Clifford Posner
Clive Bellingham
Clodie Vasli
Colin Burrow
Courtney Lilly
Craig Barney

Dan Pope
Dana Behrman
Daniel Arnold
Daniel Carpenter
Daniel Gillespie
Daniel Hahn
Daniel Hugill
Daniel Lipscombe
Daniel Venn
Daniela Steierberg
Dave Lander
Dave Rigby
David Archer
David Gould
David Hebblethwaite
David Hedges
David Higgins
David Johnson-
    Davies

David Shriver
David Smith
Dawn Hart
Dawn Mazarakis
Debbie Pinfold
Deborah Jacob
Denis Stillewagt &
    Anca Fronescu
Diana Brighouse
Dimitris Melicertes
Dominique Brocard
Duncan Marks
Duncan Ranslem

Ed Tallent
Elaine Kennedy
Elaine Rassaby
Eleanor Maier
Eleanor Walsh
Elena Traina
Eliza O'Toole
Emily Jeremiah
Emily Taylor
Emily Williams
Emily Yaewon Lee &
    Gregory Limpens
Emma Bielecki
Emma Pope
Emma Yearwood
Eric E Rubeo
Eva Hdoherty
Eva Tobler-Zumstein
Ewan Tant

Fawzia Kane
Finnuala Butler
Fiona Graham
Floriane Peycelon
Fran Sanderson
Francesca Bacigalupo
Francis Taylor

Francisco Vilhena
Friederike Knabe

G Thrower
Gabrielle Crockatt
Gavin Collins
Gawain Espley
Genevra Richardson
George Sandison &
    Daniela Laterza
George Wilkinson
Gillian Spencer
Gillian Stern
Gordon Cameron
Graham & Steph
    Parslow
Graham R Foster
Gregory Conti

Hannah Vincent
Harriet Mossop
Harriet Owles
Helen Asquith
Helen Brady
Helen Weir
Helene
    Walters-Steinberg
Henriette Heise
Henrike Laehnemann
Hugh Berkeley

Ian Barnett
Ian Kirkwood
Ian McMillan
Ignês Sodré
Irene Mansfield
Isabella Garment

J Collins
Jack Brown
Jacqueline Crooks

Jacqueline Haskell
Jacqueline Lademann
Jacqueline Taylor
Jakob Hammarskjöld
James Attlee
James Beck
James Clark
James Cubbon
James Portlock
James Scudamore
James Tierney
James Warner
James Wilper
Jamie Richards
Jamie Walsh
Jane Brandon
Jane Crookes
Jane Whiteley
Jane Woollard
Janette Ryan
Jason Spencer
Jeff Collins
Jen Hamilton-Emery
Jennifer Hearn
Jennifer Higgins
Jennifer Hurstfield
Jennifer O'Brien
Jennifer Winter
Jenny Diski
Jenny Newton
Jess Parsons
Jessica Kingsley
Jethro Soutar
Jillian Jones
Jo Harding
Joanna Flower
Joanna Luloff
Joanna Neville
Joel Love
Johan Forsell
Johannes Georg Zipp

John Allison
John Conway
John English
John Fisher
John Gent
John Hodgson
John Kelly
John Nicholson
John Royley
John Steigerwald
Jon Gower
Jonathan Ruppin
Jonathan Watkiss
Joseph Cooney
Joseph Schreiber
Joshua Davis
Josie Soutar
Judith Heneghan
Julian Duplain
Julian Lomas
Juliane Jarke
Julie Gibson
Julie Van Pelt
Juraj Janik

Kaarina Hollo
Kaite O'Reilly
Kapka Kassabova
Kate Beswick
Kate Cooper
Kate Pullinger
Kate Wild
Katharine Freeman
Katharine Robbins
Katherine El-Salahi
Katherine Wootton Joyce
Kathryn Lewis
Katie Brown
Katie Smith
Keith Dunnett

Kelly Russell
Kevin Brockmeier
Kevin Pino
Kiera Vaclavik
Kinga Burger
Kirsteen Smith
KL Ee
Kristin Pedroja
Krystalli Glyniadakis

Lana Selby
Lander Hawes
Laura Batatota
Laura Clarke
Lauren Ellemore
Leanne Bass
Leigh Vorhies
Leonie Schwab
Leri Price
Lesley Lawn
Lesley Watters
Linda Dalziel
Lindsay Brammer
Lindsay Healy
Lindsey Ford
Lissie Jacquette
Liz Clifford
Loretta Platts
Louise Bongiovanni
Louise Rogers
Lu
Lucia Rotheray
Lucie Donahue
Lucy Caldwell
Luke Healey
Lynda Graham
Lynda Ross
Lynn Martin

M Manfre
Mac York

Maeve Lambe
Maggie Livesey
Maggie Peel
Maisie & Nick Carter
Marcus Joy
Marella Oppenheim
Margaret Davis
Marie Donnelly
Marilyn Zucker
Marina Castledine
Marina Galanti
Marina Lomunno
Marion Cole
Mark Ainsbury
Mark Blacklock
Mark Lumley
Mark Waters
Martha Gifford
Martha Nicholson
Martin Brampton
Martin Hollywood
Martin Price
Mary Nash
Mary Wang
Mason Billings
Matt Oldfield
Matthew Francis
Matthew Geden
Matthew O'Dwyer
Matthew Smith
Matthew Thomas
Matthew Todd
Maureen McDermott
Maxime Dargaud-Fons
Meaghan Delahunt
Melissa
    Quignon-Finch
Melvin Davis
Michael Harrison
Michael Holtmann
Michael Johnston

Michelle Dyrness
Miranda Petruska
Mitchell Albert
Monica Hileman
Monika Olsen

Najiba
Nan Haberman
Nasser Hashmi
Natalie Smith
Natalie Wardle
Nathalie Adams
Nathan Rostron
Neil Pretty
Nicholas Laughlin
Nick James
Nick Nelson &
    Rachel Eley
Nick Sidwell
Nicola Hart
Nicola Hughes
Nina Alexandersen

Octavia Kingsley
Olivier Pynn

Pat Crowe
Pat Morgan
Patricia McCarthy
Patrick Owen
Paul Bailey
Paul Brand
Paul Jones
Paul M Cray
Paul Miller
Paul Munday
Paula Edwards
Paula McGrath
Penelope Hewett
    Brown
Peter Armstrong

Peter Burns
Peter Lockett
Peter McCambridge
Peter Murray
Peter Rowland
Peter Vos
Philbert Xavier
Philip Warren
Phyllis Reeve
Piet Van Bockstal
Piotr Kwiecinski
PM Goodman
PRAH Recordings

Rachael Williams
Rachel Kennedy
Rachel Lasserson
Rachel Matheson
Rachel Van Riel
Rachel Watkins
Read MAW Books
Rebecca Atkinson
Rebecca Braun
Rebecca Gillam
Rebecca Kershaw
Rebecca Moss
Rebecca Rosenthal
Réjane Collard
Rhiannon Armstrong
Rhodri Jones
Richard Ellis
Richard Jackson
Richard Major
Richard Smith
Rishi Dastidar
Rob Jefferson-Brown
Rob Plews
Robert Gillett
Robin Patterson
Robyn Neil
Ros Schwartz

Rose Cole
Rose Oakes
Rosemary Terry
Ross Macpherson
Roz Simpson
Ruth Diver
Ruth F Hunt
Ruth Van Driessche

S Italiano
Sabine Griffiths
Sally Baker
Sam Cunningham
Sam Gordon
Sam Ruddock
Samantha
    Sabbarton-Wright
Samantha Schnee
Samuel Alexander
    Mansfield
Sandra Hall
Sarah Benson
Sarah Butler
Sarah Duguid
Sarah Kilvington
Sarah Pybus
Sarah Salmon
Sarah Salway
Sascha Feuchert
Sasha Dugdale
Scott Beidler
SE Guine
Sean Malone
Sean McGivern
Seini O'Connor
Sez Kiss
Sheila Beirne
Shelley Krueger
Sheridan Marshall
Sigrun Hodne
Simon John Harvey

Simona Constantin
Sioned Puw Rowlands
SJ Bradley
SJ Naudé
Sonia Overall
Stephanie Carr
Stephen Bass
Stephen H Oakey
Stephen Pearsall
Steven & Gitte Evans
Steven Sidley
Sue & Ed Aldred
Sue Childs
Sue Eaglen & Colin
    Crewdson
Susan Ferguson
Susan Tomaselli
Susanna Jones
Susi Lind
Susie Roberson
Suzanne Ross
Suzy Ceulan Hughes

Tammy Watchorn
Tania Hershman
Tara Cheesman
Taylor Van Horne
Thami Fahmy
The Mighty Douche
    Softball Team
Thomas Bell
Thomas Fritz
Thomas JD Gray
Tim Jackson
Tim Theroux
Timothy Harris
Tina Rotherham-
    Winqvist
Tom Bowden
Tom Darby
Tom Franklin

Tom Mandall
Tony Bastow
Torna Russell-Hills
Trevor Lewis
Tristan Burke
Troy Zabel

Val Challen
Vanessa Jackson
Vanessa Nolan
Vasco Dones
Vicky Grut
Victoria Adams
Visaly Muthusamy
Vivien
    Doornekamp-Glass

Wendy Irvine
Wendy Langridge
Wendy Toole
Wenna Price
William G Dennehy

Yukiko Hiranuma

Zac Palmer
Zoë Brasier
Zoe Taylor

Current & Upcoming Books

Susana Moreira Marques is a writer and journalist living in Lisbon. Between 2005 and 2010 Moreira Marques lived in London, working at the BBC. She has won several prizes for her journalism, including the 2012 UNESCO 'Human Rights and Integration' Journalism Award (Portugal). *Now and at the Hour of Our Death* is her first book.

Brazilian by birth, **Julia Sanches** has lived in the United States, Mexico, Switzerland, Scotland, and Catalonia. Her translations have appeared in *Suelta*, *The Washington Review*, *Asymptote*, *Two Lines*, and *Revista Machado*. She currently lives in New York City.